Speaking CPE

Ten more practice tests for the **Cambridge C2 Proficiency**

Jane Turner

PROSPERITY EDUCATION
www.prosperityeducation.net

Registered offices: Sherlock Close, Cambridge
CB3 0HP, United Kingdom

© Prosperity Education Ltd. 2024

First published 2024

ISBN: 978-1-915654-13-7

This publication is in copyright. Subject to statutory exception
and to the provisions of relevant collective licensing agreements,
no reproduction of any part may take place without the written
permission of Prosperity Education.

'Cambridge C2 Proficiency' and 'CPE' are brands belonging to The Chancellor,
Masters and Scholars of the University of Cambridge and are not
associated with Prosperity Education or its products.

The moral rights of the author have been asserted in accordance with
the Copyright, Designs and Patents Act 1988.

For further information and resources, visit: www.prosperityeducation.net

To infinity and beyond.

Download colour test picture booklets (Part 2):

www.prosperityeducation.net/downloads

Instructions:

- Go to url
- Password: TIAB
- Select the book image
- Select content to download

Contents

Introduction 4

Test 1 7

Test 2 17

Test 3 27

Test 4 37

Test 5 47

Test 6 57

Test 7 67

Test 8 77

Test 9 87

Test 10 97

Model answers | Test 1 107

Examiner comments | Test 1 115

Introduction

Welcome to this edition of sample tests for the Cambridge C2 Proficiency Speaking examination, which has been written to replicate the Cambridge exam experience and has undergone rigorous expert and peer review.

This section of the exam is taken in pairs, or trios, of candidates, who are assessed by two examiners: the interlocutor and the assessor. The interlocutor is responsible for delivering the instructions, handling the test booklet and interacting with the candidates, while the assessor simply listens and marks each candidate's performance.

The Speaking paper is divided into three parts, each of which comprise a different task. Different degrees of participation are expected from the candidates in each of these tasks.

In **Part 1**, candidates are asked questions mainly about themselves, their background and their experiences. It starts with a set of brief introductory questions (e.g. ...*and your names are? Where are you from?*) and continues with one or more topic-based questions. These topics may include things like holidays and travel, leisure-time activities, friends and family, television, etc. In responding to these questions, candidates are expected to provide brief but complete answers.

Timing	2 minutes (pair) / 3 minutes (trio)
Focus	Giving personal information, expressing opinions about various topics, and talking about past experiences and plans for the future.
Interaction	Interlocutor – Candidate

Part 2, which is divided into two tasks, is the main collaborative part of the test. In this part, candidates are expected to have a two-way conversation during which they should exchange views, opinions and information through collaboration and negotiation. For the first task, candidates are given several photographs and are asked to react to two of them based on some brief instructions (e.g. ...*look at pictures * and * and talk together about how common these situations are when going on a trip*). Candidates have one minute to speak together. In the second task, which lasts three minutes, candidates are presented with a hypothetical situation in which the images or their topics represent something important. Candidates are then asked to develop a three-minute discussion about what all the pictures represent, and to make a decision or put forward a suggestion based on their discussion.

Timing	Total: 4 minutes (pair) / 6 minutes (trio) Task 1 – Introductory discussion: 1 minute (pair) / 2 minutes (trio) Task 2 – Long discussion: 3 minutes (pair) / 4 minutes (trio)
Focus	Discussing, exchanging ideas, agreeing and disagreeing, asking for opinions, explaining views, justifying opinions, reaching agreements, making decisions, suggesting ideas, speculating, negotiating, etc.
Interaction	Interlocutor – Candidate – Candidate

Part 3, which also comprises two different tasks, is the main 'individual' part of the exam, although there some candidate interaction is still expected. Also, it is important to know that this entire part revolves around one core topic (e.g. *Trust*). In the first task, one of the candidates is given a card with a question and three prompts. He/she is then asked to talk about the topic on the card for about two minutes. When the two minutes are over, a short discussion will begin. The examiner will ask the second candidate a follow-up question, and then invite the first candidate to join in too (e.g. *What do you think?*). After approximately one minute, it is the other candidate's turn to be given a card, and the task will begin again.

After both turns are over, the examiner will move on to the last task of the test, which consists of a set of questions that stem from the main discussion topic (e.g. *Trust*). The candidates are expected to develop extended answers, and may be prompted to exchange views rather than answer individually.

Timing	Total: 10 minutes (pair) / 15 minutes (trio)
	Task 1 – Long turn: 2 minutes (per candidate's turn)
	Task 2 – Short discussion: 1 minute (per candidate's turn)
	Task 3 – Final discussion: 4 minutes
Focus	Imparting information, organising longer speech, expressing and justifying opinions, agreeing and disagreeing, evaluating, etc.
Interaction	Interlocutor – Candidate – Candidate

This book aims to provide meaningful speaking practice while following the format of the C2 Proficiency Speaking paper. Model answers and examiner comments are provided for Test 1, allowing both teachers and candidates to familiarise themselves with the format and level of the exam, and the type of questions and topics covered. Furthermore, and most importantly, students can learn, through repetitive practice, what to expect on the day of their Speaking test.

I hope that you will find this resource a useful study aid, and I wish you all the best in preparing for the C2 Proficiency examination.

Jane Turner
Cambridge, 2024

Jane Turner is an associate lecturer in EAP/EFL at Anglia Ruskin University, Cambridge, and an EFL materials writer for international exam boards, universities and publishers. She previously worked as a Cambridge ESOL examiner for the British Council, and holds an MA in Educational Management and Cambridge CELTA and DELTA.

Cambridge C2 Proficiency Speaking

Test 1

Test 1 – Part 1
2 minutes (3 minutes for groups of three)

Cambridge C2 Proficiency: Speaking

Candidates' background

Interlocutor Good morning/afternoon/evening. My name is …………… and this is my colleague ……………. .

And your names are?

Could I have your mark sheets, please?

Thank you.

First of all, we'd like to know something about you.

- **Where are you from** *(Candidate A)*? **And you** *(Candidate B)*?
- *[Address Candidate B]* **Are you working or studying at the moment?**
- *[Address Candidate A]* **And you?**

Select a further question for each candidate:

- Would you describe yourself as creative? …… (Why? / Why not?)
- What sort of work would you like to do in the future? …… (Why?)
- Do you think you spend too much time using social media? …… (Why? / Why not?)
- How do you like to celebrate special occasions?
- What activities do you find relaxing? …… (Why?)
- If you had the power to change something about where you live, what would you change? …… (Why?)

Candidates

………………………………………………………………………

Interlocutor Thank you.

Cambridge C2 Proficiency: Speaking	Test 1 – Part 2
	4 minutes (6 minutes for groups of three)

1 Report – mass tourism

Interlocutor Now, in this part of the test you're going to do something together. Here are some pictures of people in different situations.

*Place **Part 2** booklet in front of the candidates. Select **two** of the pictures for the candidates to look at.*

First, I'd like you to look at pictures and talk together about the potential impacts of mass tourism on local communities.

You have about a minute for this, so don't worry if I interrupt you.

Candidates

1 minute (2 minutes for groups of three)

Interlocutor Thank you. Now look at all the pictures.

I'd like you to imagine that a committee is writing a report about the pros and cons of bringing mass tourism to the local area. These pictures will be used in the report to show some of the problems associated with mass tourism.

Talk together about what can be done locally to address the issues that these pictures show. Then decide which of these issues should be the main focus of the committee's report.

You have about three minutes to talk about this.

Candidates

Approximately 3 minutes (4 minutes for groups of three)

Interlocutor Thank you. (Can I have the booklet, please?) *Retrieve **Part 2** booklet.*

Test 1 – Part 2
Booklet

Cambridge C2 Proficiency: Speaking

1. Report – mass tourism

Test 1 – Part 3
Approximately 10 minutes

Cambridge C2 Proficiency: Speaking

Leadership

Interlocutor	Now, in this part of the test you're each going to talk on your own for about two minutes. You need to listen while your partner is speaking because you'll be asked to comment afterwards.
	So *(Candidate A)*, I'm going to give you a card with a question written on it and I'd like you to tell us what you think. There are also some ideas on the card for you to use if you like.
	All right? Here is your card.
	*Place **Part 3** booklet, open at **Task 1(a)**, in front of Candidate A.*
	Please let *(Candidate B)* **see your card. Remember** *(Candidate A)*, **you have about two minutes to talk before we join in.**
	Allow up to 10 seconds before saying, if necessary: **Would you like to begin now?**
Candidate A	.... *2 minutes*
Interlocutor	**Thank you.**
Interlocutor	*Ask **one** of the following questions to Candidate B:* • Are the same leadership skills necessary in every situation? (Why? / Why not?) • What difficulties can arise when making the transition from team member to team leader? • What are the most effective ways to develop leadership skills?

> *Invite Candidate A to join in by selecting one of the following prompts:*
> • What do you think?
> • Do you agree?
> • How about you?

Candidates	.... *1 minute*
Interlocutor	**Thank you. (Can I have the booklet, please?)** *Retrieve **Part 3** booklet.*

Task 1(a)

What qualities make an effective leader?

• communication

• vision

• decision making

| Test 1 – Part 3 | Cambridge C2 Proficiency: Speaking |

Leadership – continued

Interlocutor Now *(Candidate B)*, **it's your turn to be given a question. Here is your card.**

*Place **Part 3** booklet, open at **Task 1(b)**, in front of Candidate B.*

Please let *(Candidate A)* **see your card. Remember** *(Candidate B)*, **you have about two minutes to tell us what you think, and there are some ideas on the card for you to use if you like. All right?**

Allow up to 10 seconds before saying, if necessary: **Would you like to begin now?**

Candidate B

2 minutes

Interlocutor Thank you.

Interlocutor *Ask **one** of the following questions to Candidate A:*
- **To what extent do leaders have to be ruthless? (Why?)**
- **How can leaders persuade people to do what they want?**
- **What makes leadership difficult? (Why?)**

> *Invite Candidate B to join in by selecting one of the following prompts:*
> - **What do you think?**
> - **Do you agree?**
> - **How about you?**

Candidates

1 minute

Interlocutor Thank you. **(Can I have the booklet, please?)** *Retrieve **Part 3** booklet.*

Task 1(b)

Why does leadership appeal to some people?

• status

• making a difference

• autonomy

| Test 1 – Part 3 | Cambridge C2 Proficiency: Speaking |

Leadership – continued

Interlocutor   Now, to finish the test, we're going to talk about 'leadership' in general.

Address a selection of the following questions to both candidates:

- Do you think leaders are born or made? (Why? / Why not?)
- Some people say that role models and leaders are different things. What do you think?
- In general, do you think leaders get enough respect in society? (Why / why not?)
- It is sometimes said that the most effective leaders are invisible. Do you agree? (Why? / Why not?)
- Is being popular a must for leaders? (Why? / Why not?)
- How useful is it for leaders to have an understanding of psychology? (Why?)

Interlocutor   Thank you. That is the end of the test.

Mark sheet

Date | DD | MM | YY |

Candidate _____

Marks available

Grammatical Resource	0	1	1.5	2	2.5	3	3.5	4	4.5	5
Lexical Resource	0	1	1.5	2	2.5	3	3.5	4	4.5	5
Discourse Management	0	1	1.5	2	2.5	3	3.5	4	4.5	5
Pronunciation	0	1	1.5	2	2.5	3	3.5	4	4.5	5
Interactive Communication	0	1	1.5	2	2.5	3	3.5	4	4.5	5
Global Achievement	0	1	1.5	2	2.5	3	3.5	4	4.5	5

Item descriptors

Grammatical Resource *Control* *Range*	• Degree of control of grammatical forms. • Range of grammatical forms used.
Lexical Resource *Range* *Appropriacy*	• Range of vocabulary used to give and exchange views. • Appropriacy of vocabulary used.
Discourse Management *Extent* *Relevance* *Coherence* *Cohesion*	• Stretches of language produced. • Relevance of contributions and organisation of ideas. • Use of appropriate cohesive devices and discourse markers.
Pronunciation *Intonation* *Stress* *Individual sounds*	• Intelligibility • Intonation • Word stress • Individual sounds
Interactive Communication *Initiating* *Responding* *Development*	• Initiating, responding and linking contributions to other speakers' interventions. • Maintaining and developing interaction, and negotiating towards an outcome. • Widening the scope of the interaction.

Cambridge C2 Proficiency Speaking

Test 2

Test 2 – Part 1
2 minutes (3 minutes for groups of three)

Cambridge C2 Proficiency: Speaking

Candidates' background

Interlocutor Good morning/afternoon/evening. My name is ………….. and this is my colleague …………… .

And your names are?

Could I have your mark sheets, please?

Thank you.

First of all, we'd like to know something about you.

- **Where are you from** *(Candidate A)*? **And you** *(Candidate B)*?
- *[Address Candidate B]* **Are you working or studying at the moment?**
- *[Address Candidate A]* **And you?**

Select a further question for each candidate:

- **Can you tell us something about where you live?**
- **What sort of job do you imagine doing in the future? …… (Why?)**
- **What is your idea of a fun day out? …… (Why?)**
- **How would you describe your personal sense of style?**
- **Would you rather have a few close friends or a large network of acquaintances? …… (Why?)**
- **If you had the time to take up a new hobby, what would you like to try? …… (Why?)**

Candidates

Interlocutor Thank you.

Cambridge C2 Proficiency: Speaking	Test 2 – Part 2
	4 minutes (6 minutes for groups of three)

1 School project – charity fundraising

Interlocutor Now, in this part of the test you're going to do something together. Here are some pictures of people in different situations.

*Place **Part 2** booklet in front of the candidates. Select **two** of the pictures for the candidates to look at.*

First, I'd like you to look at pictures and talk together about the charitable causes that tend to get the most support from the public.

You have about a minute for this, so don't worry if I interrupt you.

Candidates

....
1 minute (2 minutes for groups of three)

Interlocutor Thank you. Now look at all the pictures.

I'd like you to imagine that your school has asked to you come up with ways to raise funds for a good cause in the local area. These pictures show some common ways that people can raise funds for charity.

Talk together about the most important considerations to bear in mind when planning a fundraising campaign. Then decide which of these methods would be the most effective means of fundraising.

You have about three minutes to talk about this.

Candidates

....
Approximately 3 minutes (4 minutes for groups of three)

Interlocutor Thank you. (Can I have the booklet, please?) *Retrieve **Part 2** booklet.*

Test 2 – Part 2
Booklet

Cambridge C2 Proficiency: Speaking

1 School project – charity fundraising

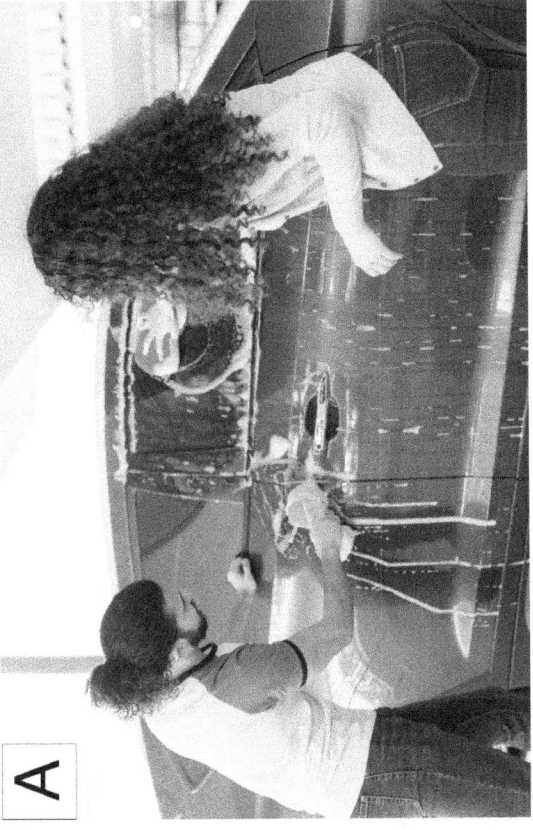

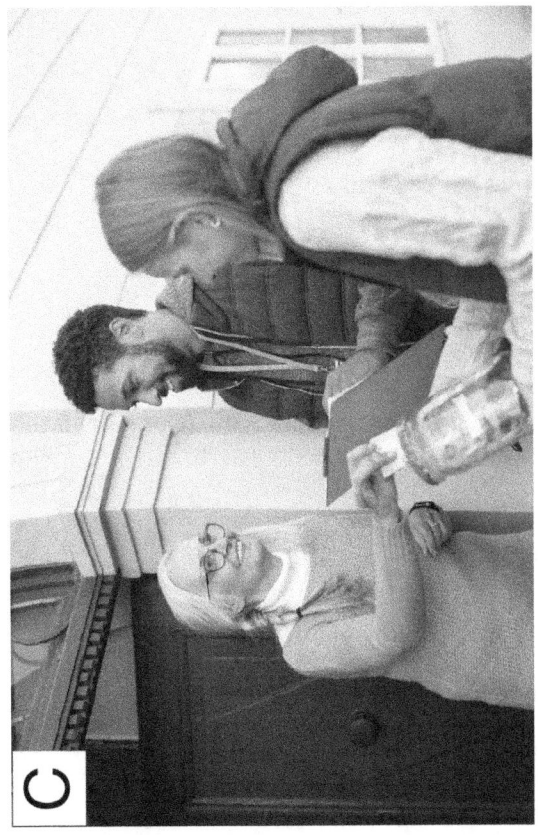

Test 2 – Part 3	Cambridge C2 Proficiency: Speaking
Approximately 10 minutes	

The Music Industry

Interlocutor	Now, in this part of the test you're each going to talk on your own for about two minutes. You need to listen while your partner is speaking because you'll be asked to comment afterwards. So *(Candidate A)*, I'm going to give you a card with a question written on it and I'd like you to tell us what you think. There are also some ideas on the card for you to use if you like. All right? Here is your card. *Place **Part 3** booklet, open at **Task 1(a)**, in front of Candidate A.* **Please let** *(Candidate B)* **see your card. Remember** *(Candidate A)*, **you have about two minutes to talk before we join in.** *Allow up to 10 seconds before saying, if necessary:* **Would you like to begin now?**
Candidate A	.... *2 minutes*
Interlocutor	Thank you.
Interlocutor	*Ask **one** of the following questions to Candidate B:* • How important is live performance for building an artist's reputation? (Why?) • Should musicians use their fame to discuss social issues? (Why / why not?) • What could be done to protect new artists about to enter the music industry?

> *Invite Candidate A to join in by selecting one of the following prompts:*
> • **What do you think?**
> • **Do you agree?**
> • **How about you?**

Candidates	.... *1 minute*
Interlocutor	Thank you. (Can I have the booklet, please?) *Retrieve **Part 3** booklet.*

Task 1(a)

How has the music industry changed in the last two decades?

• how people consume music

• musicians' paths to success

• multicultural music scenes

| Test 2 – Part 3 | Cambridge C2 Proficiency: Speaking |

The Music Industry – continued

Interlocutor	Now *(Candidate B)*, it's your turn to be given a question. Here is your card.

*Place **Part 3** booklet, open at **Task 1(b)**, in front of Candidate B.*

Please let *(Candidate A)* **see your card. Remember** *(Candidate B)*, **you have about two minutes to tell us what you think, and there are some ideas on the card for you to use if you like. All right?**

Allow up to 10 seconds before saying, if necessary: **Would you like to begin now?**

Candidate B	

2 minutes

Interlocutor	Thank you.

Interlocutor	*Ask **one** of the following questions to Candidate A:*

- Should record companies control how their artists look or dress? (Why? / Why not?)
- How do record companies promote new artists?
- Should fans be allowed to record live performances when they go to concerts? (Why / why not?)

> *Invite Candidate B to join in by selecting one of the following prompts:*
> - **What do you think?**
> - **Do you agree?**
> - **How about you?**

Candidates	

1 minute

Interlocutor	Thank you. (Can I have the booklet, please?) *Retrieve Part 3 booklet.*

Task 1(b)

What pitfalls might artists face in the music industry?

• knowing who to trust

• balancing creativity and commercial interests

• handling fame

Test 2 – Part 3   **Cambridge C2 Proficiency: Speaking**

The Music Industry – continued

Interlocutor   Now, to finish the test, we're going to talk about 'the music industry' in general.

Address a selection of the following questions to both candidates:

- Do you think the music industry treats artists well? (Why? / Why not?)
- Some people say that downloading music is destroying the music industry. What do you think?
- Do TV talent shows like 'Pop Idol' help or hinder the music industry? (Why?)
- It is sometimes said that some musical genres are more progressive than others. Do you agree? (Why? / Why not?)
- To what extent might AI change the music industry? (Why?)
- Can an artist become successful without compromising their artist ideals? (Why? / Why not?)

Interlocutor   Thank you. That is the end of the test.

Mark sheet

| Date | DD | MM | YY | | Candidate | _____ |

Marks available

Grammatical Resource	0	1	1.5	2	2.5	3	3.5	4	4.5	5
Lexical Resource	0	1	1.5	2	2.5	3	3.5	4	4.5	5
Discourse Management	0	1	1.5	2	2.5	3	3.5	4	4.5	5
Pronunciation	0	1	1.5	2	2.5	3	3.5	4	4.5	5
Interactive Communication	0	1	1.5	2	2.5	3	3.5	4	4.5	5
Global Achievement	0	1	1.5	2	2.5	3	3.5	4	4.5	5

Item descriptors

Grammatical Resource *Control* *Range*	• Degree of control of grammatical forms. • Range of grammatical forms used.
Lexical Resource *Range* *Appropriacy*	• Range of vocabulary used to give and exchange views. • Appropriacy of vocabulary used.
Discourse Management *Extent* *Relevance* *Coherence* *Cohesion*	• Stretches of language produced. • Relevance of contributions and organisation of ideas. • Use of appropriate cohesive devices and discourse markers.
Pronunciation *Intonation* *Stress* *Individual sounds*	• Intelligibility • Intonation • Word stress • Individual sounds
Interactive Communication *Initiating* *Responding* *Development*	• Initiating, responding and linking contributions to other speakers' interventions. • Maintaining and developing interaction, and negotiating towards an outcome. • Widening the scope of the interaction.

Cambridge C2 Proficiency Speaking

Test 3

Test 3 – Part 1
2 minutes (3 minutes for groups of three)

Cambridge C2 Proficiency: Speaking

Candidates' background

Interlocutor Good morning/afternoon/evening. My name is …………… and this is my colleague …………… .

And your names are?

Could I have your mark sheets, please?

Thank you.

First of all, we'd like to know something about you.

- **Where are you from** *(Candidate A)*? **And you** *(Candidate B)*?
- *[Address Candidate B]* **Are you working or studying at the moment?**
- *[Address Candidate A]* **And you?**

Select a further question for each candidate:

- **What methods do you like to use to help you learn new skills?** …… **(Why?)**
- **Would you describe yourself as a 'foodie'?** …… **(Why? / Why not?)**
- **Can you tell us about a person that has inspired you?**
- **Do you prefer early mornings or late nights?** …… **(Why?)**
- **Do you work to live or live to work?** …… **(Why?)**
- **If you could travel back in time, which era or place would you visit?** …… **(Why?)**

Candidates

……………………………………………………………………

Interlocutor Thank you.

Cambridge C2 Proficiency: Speaking

Test 3 – Part 2
4 minutes (6 minutes for groups of three)

1 Marketing campaign – promoting a university

Interlocutor Now, in this part of the test you're going to do something together. Here are some pictures of different situations.

*Place **Part 2** booklet in front of the candidates. Select **two** of the pictures for the candidates to look at.*

First, I'd like you to look at pictures and talk together about the different reasons many people value a university education.

You have about a minute for this, so don't worry if I interrupt you.

Candidates

1 minute (2 minutes for groups of three)

Interlocutor Thank you. Now look at all the pictures.

I'd like you to imagine that a university is planning a marketing campaign which aims to raise the profile of the university. These pictures show some of the concepts the university wants to highlight.

Talk together about what the concepts shown in the pictures say about the university. Then decide which of these concepts should **NOT** be the main focus of the university's marketing campaign.

You have about three minutes to talk about this.

Candidates

Approximately 3 minutes (4 minutes for groups of three)

Interlocutor Thank you. (Can I have the booklet, please?) *Retrieve **Part 2** booklet.*

Test 3 – Part 2
Booklet

Cambridge C2 Proficiency: Speaking

1 Marketing campaign – promoting a university

Test 3 – Part 3
Approximately 10 minutes

Cambridge C2 Proficiency: Speaking

Transport and Traffic Congestion

| Interlocutor | Now, in this part of the test you're each going to talk on your own for about two minutes. You need to listen while your partner is speaking because you'll be asked to comment afterwards.

So *(Candidate A)*, I'm going to give you a card with a question written on it and I'd like you to tell us what you think. There are also some ideas on the card for you to use if you like.

All right? Here is your card.

*Place **Part 3** booklet, open at **Task 1(a)**, in front of Candidate A.*

Please let *(Candidate B)* **see your card. Remember** *(Candidate A)*, **you have about two minutes to talk before we join in.**

Allow up to 10 seconds before saying, if necessary: **Would you like to begin now?** |

Candidate A

....
2 minutes

| Interlocutor | Thank you. |

| Interlocutor | *Ask **one** of the following questions to Candidate B:*
• **Generally speaking, are you satisfied with the public transport where you live? (Why? / Why not?)**
• **Do you think you are a considerate driver or passenger? (Why? / Why not?)**
• **Do you think cars can be beautiful? (Why? / Why not?)** |

> *Invite Candidate A to join in by selecting one of the following prompts:*
> • **What do you think?**
> • **Do you agree?**
> • **How about you?**

Candidates

....
1 minute

| Interlocutor | **Thank you. (Can I have the booklet, please?)** *Retrieve **Part 3** booklet.* |

Task 1(a)

Which factors do people consider when choosing a mode of transport?

• **convenience**

• **cost**

• **the environment**

Test 3 – Part 3   Cambridge C2 Proficiency: Speaking

Transport and Traffic Congestion – continued

Interlocutor	Now *(Candidate B)*, **it's your turn to be given a question. Here is your card.**

*Place **Part 3** booklet, open at **Task 1(b)**, in front of Candidate B.*

Please let *(Candidate A)* **see your card. Remember** *(Candidate B)*, **you have about two minutes to tell us what you think, and there are some ideas on the card for you to use if you like. All right?**

Allow up to 10 seconds before saying, if necessary: **Would you like to begin now?**

Candidate B

2 minutes

Interlocutor   Thank you.

Interlocutor   *Ask **one** of the following questions to Candidate A:*
- **Is having an expensive car a desirable status symbol? (Why? / Why not?)**
- **Do you think young people should pay more for car insurance? (Why? / Why not?)**
- **Generally speaking, where is driving more difficult: cities or rural areas? (Why?)**

> *Invite Candidate B to join in by selecting one of the following prompts:*
> - **What do you think?**
> - **Do you agree?**
> - **How about you?**

Candidates

1 minute

Interlocutor   Thank you. (Can I have the booklet, please?) *Retrieve **Part 3** booklet.*

Task 1(b)

What are the potential implications of banning cars from a town centre?

- **parking**
- **economy**
- **pollution**

Transport and Traffic Congestion – continued

Interlocutor Now, to finish the test, we're going to talk about 'transport' in general.

Address a selection of the following questions to both candidates:

- What could be done to make travelling by public transport a more pleasant experience? (Why?)
- Is remote working the best solution to traffic congestion? (Why? / Why not?)
- In many countries, Transport Minister is a relatively low-profile governmental position. What do you think about this?
- Who should be entitled to use public transport for free? (Why?)
- What role does technology play in addressing traffic congestion?
- What are some common features of car advertising on TV?

Interlocutor Thank you. That is the end of the test.

Mark sheet

Date | DD | MM | YY

Candidate _____

Marks available

Grammatical Resource	0	1	1.5	2	2.5	3	3.5	4	4.5	5
Lexical Resource	0	1	1.5	2	2.5	3	3.5	4	4.5	5
Discourse Management	0	1	1.5	2	2.5	3	3.5	4	4.5	5
Pronunciation	0	1	1.5	2	2.5	3	3.5	4	4.5	5
Interactive Communication	0	1	1.5	2	2.5	3	3.5	4	4.5	5
Global Achievement	0	1	1.5	2	2.5	3	3.5	4	4.5	5

Item descriptors

Grammatical Resource *Control* *Range*	• Degree of control of grammatical forms. • Range of grammatical forms used.
Lexical Resource *Range* *Appropriacy*	• Range of vocabulary used to give and exchange views. • Appropriacy of vocabulary used.
Discourse Management *Extent* *Relevance* *Coherence* *Cohesion*	• Stretches of language produced. • Relevance of contributions and organisation of ideas. • Use of appropriate cohesive devices and discourse markers.
Pronunciation *Intonation* *Stress* *Individual sounds*	• Intelligibility • Intonation • Word stress • Individual sounds
Interactive Communication *Initiating* *Responding* *Development*	• Initiating, responding and linking contributions to other speakers' interventions. • Maintaining and developing interaction, and negotiating towards an outcome. • Widening the scope of the interaction.

Cambridge C2 Proficiency Speaking

Test 4

Test 4 – Part 1	Cambridge C2 Proficiency: Speaking
2 minutes (3 minutes for groups of three)	

Candidates' background

Interlocutor Good morning/afternoon/evening. My name is …………. and this is my colleague …………. .

And your names are?

Could I have your mark sheets, please?

Thank you.

First of all, we'd like to know something about you.

- **Where are you from** *(Candidate A)*? **And you** *(Candidate B)*?
- *[Address Candidate B]* **Are you working or studying at the moment?**
- *[Address Candidate A]* **And you?**

Select a further question for each candidate:

- **Can you tell us about a subject that you would like to learn more about? …… (Why?)**
- **What do you imagine doing in ten years' time? …… (Why?)**
- **What do you appreciate most about the place where you're from? …… (Why?)**
- **What is your attitude towards money and finances? …… (Why?)**
- **Can you describe an interesting place you have visited?**
- **If you could meet a famous person, who would you choose? …… (Why?)**

Candidates

………………………………………………………………………

Interlocutor Thank you.

Cambridge C2 Proficiency: Speaking	Test 4 – Part 2
	4 minutes (6 minutes for groups of three)

1 **Competition – city of cultural significance**

Interlocutor Now, in this part of the test you're going to do something together. Here are some pictures of people in different situations.

*Place **Part 2** booklet in front of the candidates. Select **two** of the pictures for the candidates to look at.*

First, I'd like you to look at pictures and talk together about how communities benefit from having access to cultural facilities.

You have about a minute for this, so don't worry if I interrupt you.

Candidates

1 minute (2 minutes for groups of three)

Interlocutor **Thank you. Now look at all the pictures.**

I'd like you to imagine that a city is bidding to gain official recognition as a "City of Cultural Significance". These pictures show some ideas of what the city is planning to highlight in its bid.

Talk together about what potential benefits the city may gain if its bid is successful. Then decide which of these images is most likely to generate interest in the city.

You have about three minutes to talk about this.

Candidates

Approximately 3 minutes (4 minutes for groups of three)

Interlocutor **Thank you. (Can I have the booklet, please?)** *Retrieve **Part 2** booklet.*

Test 4 – Part 2
Booklet

Cambridge C2 Proficiency: Speaking

1 Competition – city of cultural significance

Test 4 – Part 3
Approximately 10 minutes

Cambridge C2 Proficiency: Speaking

Attitudes to Food

Interlocutor	Now, in this part of the test you're each going to talk on your own for about two minutes. You need to listen while your partner is speaking because you'll be asked to comment afterwards.
	So *(Candidate A)*, I'm going to give you a card with a question written on it and I'd like you to tell us what you think. There are also some ideas on the card for you to use if you like.
	All right? Here is your card.
	*Place **Part 3** booklet, open at **Task 1(a)**, in front of Candidate A.*
	Please let *(Candidate B)* **see your card. Remember** *(Candidate A)*, **you have about two minutes to talk before we join in.**
	Allow up to 10 seconds before saying, if necessary: **Would you like to begin now?**
Candidate A	.... *2 minutes*
Interlocutor	Thank you.
Interlocutor	*Ask **one** of the following questions to Candidate B:* • Do you prefer trying new places or eating at favourite restaurant? (Why?) • To what extent are you influenced by restaurant reviews? (Why?) • Is being a chef considered a prestigious job in your country? (Why? / Why not?)

> *Invite Candidate A to join in by selecting one of the following prompts:*
> • **What do you think?**
> • **Do you agree?**
> • **How about you?**

Candidates	.... *1 minute*
Interlocutor	**Thank you. (Can I have the booklet, please?)** *Retrieve **Part 3** booklet.*

Task 1(a)

How do restaurants retain loyal customers?

• **atmosphere**

• **value for money**

• **menu options**

| Test 4 – Part 3 | Cambridge C2 Proficiency: Speaking |

Attitudes to Food – continued

| Interlocutor | Now *(Candidate B)*, **it's your turn to be given a question. Here is your card.** |

*Place **Part 3** booklet, open at **Task 1(b)**, in front of Candidate B.*

Please let *(Candidate A)* **see your card. Remember** *(Candidate B)*, **you have about two minutes to tell us what you think, and there are some ideas on the card for you to use if you like. All right?**

Allow up to 10 seconds before saying, if necessary: **Would you like to begin now?**

Candidate B

2 minutes

| Interlocutor | Thank you. |

| Interlocutor | *Ask **one** of the following questions to Candidate A:* |

- **Do you prefer following recipes or experimenting in the kitchen? (Why?)**
- **In your country, what do schools teach their pupils about food and cooking?**
- **Has fast food had a negative impact in the restaurant industry in your country? (Why? / Why not?)**

> *Invite Candidate B to join in by selecting one of the following prompts:*
> - **What do you think?**
> - **Do you agree?**
> - **How about you?**

Candidates

1 minute

| Interlocutor | Thank you. (Can I have the booklet, please?) *Retrieve Part 3 booklet.* |

Task 1(b)

What inspires people to develop their knowledge of food?

• **travel**

• **TV**

• **food trends**

Test 4 – Part 3 — Cambridge C2 Proficiency: Speaking

Attitudes to Food – continued

Interlocutor Now, to finish the test, we're going to talk about 'attitudes to food' in general.

Address a selection of the following questions to both candidates:

- What role does psychology play in people's food preferences? (Why?)
- What might make people reluctant to prepare healthy food?
- Some people say that governments should introduce higher taxes on unhealthy food and drinks. What do you think?
- How have people's eating habits changed in the past two decades. (Why?)
- In general, do you think it is important to protect national food traditions? (Why / why not?)
- What difficult issues might the food industry face in the future?

Interlocutor Thank you. That is the end of the test.

Mark sheet

Date | DD | MM | YY

Candidate _____

Marks available

Grammatical Resource	0	1	1.5	2	2.5	3	3.5	4	4.5	5
Lexical Resource	0	1	1.5	2	2.5	3	3.5	4	4.5	5
Discourse Management	0	1	1.5	2	2.5	3	3.5	4	4.5	5
Pronunciation	0	1	1.5	2	2.5	3	3.5	4	4.5	5
Interactive Communication	0	1	1.5	2	2.5	3	3.5	4	4.5	5
Global Achievement	0	1	1.5	2	2.5	3	3.5	4	4.5	5

Item descriptors

Grammatical Resource *Control* *Range*	• Degree of control of grammatical forms. • Range of grammatical forms used.
Lexical Resource *Range* *Appropriacy*	• Range of vocabulary used to give and exchange views. • Appropriacy of vocabulary used.
Discourse Management *Extent* *Relevance* *Coherence* *Cohesion*	• Stretches of language produced. • Relevance of contributions and organisation of ideas. • Use of appropriate cohesive devices and discourse markers.
Pronunciation *Intonation* *Stress* *Individual sounds*	• Intelligibility • Intonation • Word stress • Individual sounds
Interactive Communication *Initiating* *Responding* *Development*	• Initiating, responding and linking contributions to other speakers' interventions. • Maintaining and developing interaction, and negotiating towards an outcome. • Widening the scope of the interaction.

Cambridge C2 Proficiency Speaking

Test 5

Test 5 – Part 1	Cambridge C2 Proficiency: Speaking
2 minutes (3 minutes for groups of three)	

Candidates' background

Interlocutor Good morning/afternoon/evening. My name is .... and this is my colleague ....

And your names are?

Could I have your mark sheets, please?

Thank you.

First of all, we'd like to know something about you.

- **Where are you from** *(Candidate A)*? **And you** *(Candidate B)*?
- *[Address Candidate B]* **Are you working or studying at the moment?**
- *[Address Candidate A]* **And you?**

Select a further question for each candidate:

- Is (candidate's town / area) a good place for nature lovers? ...... (Why? / Why not?)
- What type of social events do you enjoy the most? ...... (Why?)
- What in your life would you like to spend less time doing? ...... (Why?)
- Can you tell us about an important piece of advice you've received?
- How important is travel to you? ...... (Why?)
- What personal trait do you most admire in other people? ...... (Why?)

Candidates

Interlocutor Thank you.

Cambridge C2 Proficiency: Speaking

Test 5 – Part 2
4 minutes (6 minutes for groups of three)

1 **Academic conference – scientific research**

Interlocutor Now, in this part of the test you're going to do something together. Here are some pictures of people in different situations.

*Place **Part 2** booklet in front of the candidates. Select **two** of the pictures for the candidates to look at.*

First, I'd like you to look at pictures and talk together about how much of a priority these issues are for your country.

You have about a minute for this, so don't worry if I interrupt you.

Candidates

1 minute (2 minutes for groups of three)

Interlocutor Thank you. Now look at all the pictures.

I'd like you to imagine that a university is organising an academic conference about the social impacts of scientific research. These pictures show some of the subjects that are being considered for the conference.

Talk together about the potential implications of the issues that these pictures show. Then decide which of these issues should be the main focus of the conference.

You have about three minutes to talk about this.

Candidates

Approximately 3 minutes (4 minutes for groups of three)

Interlocutor Thank you. (Can I have the booklet, please?) *Retrieve **Part 2** booklet.*

Test 5 – Part 2
Booklet

Cambridge C2 Proficiency: Speaking

1 Academic conference – scientific research

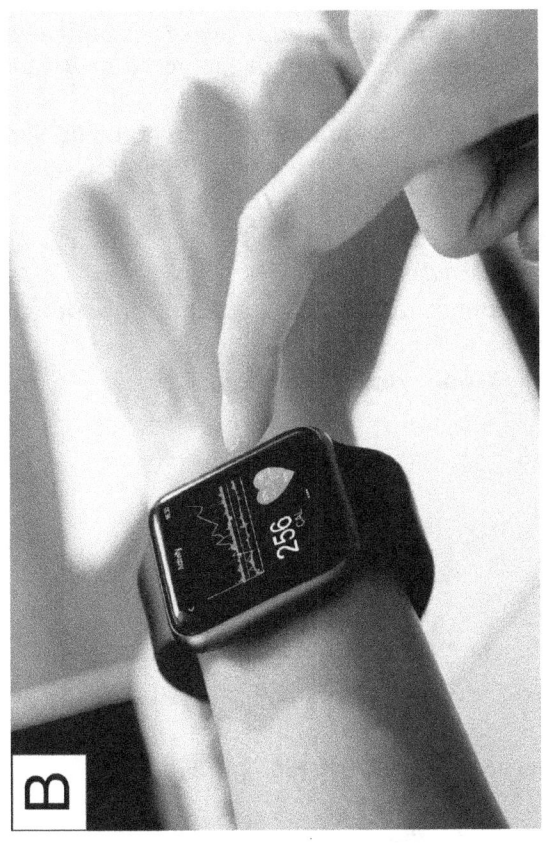

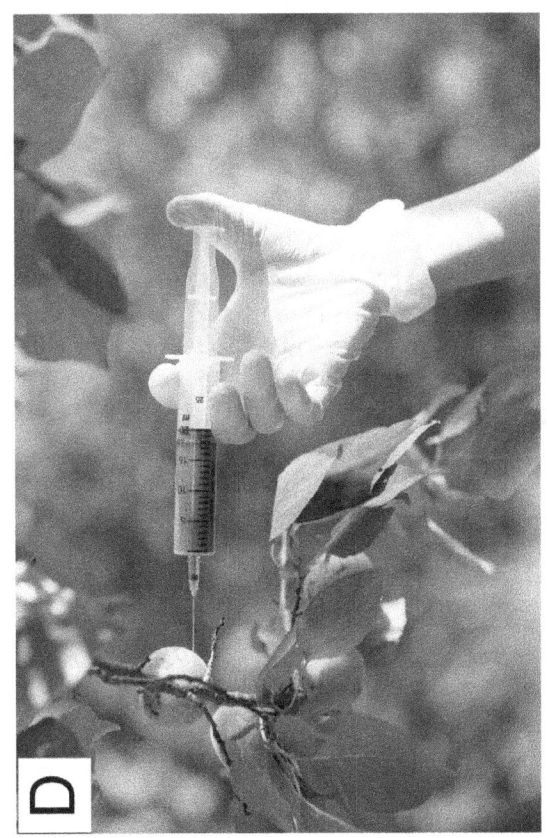

Test 5 – Part 3	Cambridge C2 Proficiency: Speaking
Approximately 10 minutes	

Media Influence

Interlocutor	Now, in this part of the test you're each going to talk on your own for about two minutes. You need to listen while your partner is speaking because you'll be asked to comment afterwards.
	So *(Candidate A)*, I'm going to give you a card with a question written on it and I'd like you to tell us what you think. There are also some ideas on the card for you to use if you like.
	All right? Here is your card.
	*Place **Part 3** booklet, open at **Task 1(a)**, in front of Candidate A.*
	Please let *(Candidate B)* **see your card. Remember** *(Candidate A)*, **you have about two minutes to talk before we join in.**
	Allow up to 10 seconds before saying, if necessary: **Would you like to begin now?**

Candidate A

....
2 minutes

Interlocutor	Thank you.
Interlocutor	*Ask **one** of the following questions to Candidate B:*
	• Do you ever post about news stories or current affairs online? (Why? / Why not?)
	• Do media interviews change your perceptions of a public figure? (Why? / Why not?)
	• Would you make a good journalist? Why? / Why not?)

> *Invite Candidate A to join in by selecting one of the following prompts:*
> - **What do you think?**
> - **Do you agree?**
> - **How about you?**

Candidates

....
1 minute

Interlocutor	**Thank you. (Can I have the booklet, please?)** *Retrieve **Part 3** booklet.*

Task 1(a)

How has the development of social media changed the news industry?

• consumer engagement

• target audiences

• reliability of information

Test 5 – Part 3   Cambridge C2 Proficiency: Speaking

Media influence – continued

Interlocutor Now *(Candidate B)*, **it's your turn to be given a question. Here is your card.**

*Place **Part 3** booklet, open at **Task 1(b)**, in front of Candidate B.*

Please let *(Candidate A)* **see your card. Remember** *(Candidate B)*, **you have about two minutes to tell us what you think, and there are some ideas on the card for you to use if you like. All right?**

Allow up to 10 seconds before saying, if necessary: **Would you like to begin now?**

Candidate B

....

2 minutes

Interlocutor Thank you.

Interlocutor *Ask **one** of the following questions to Candidate A:*
- **In general, where do you get most of your information about current affairs? (Why?)**
- **To what extent do you think the media in your country is trustworthy? (Why?)**
- **What can you tell about a person based on the newspaper they read?**

> *Invite Candidate B to join in by selecting one of the following prompts:*
> - **What do you think?**
> - **Do you agree?**
> - **How about you?**

Candidates

....

1 minute

Interlocutor Thank you. (Can I have the booklet, please?) *Retrieve **Part 3** booklet.*

Task 1(b)

To what extent does the media influence public life?

- politics
- trends
- role models

Test 5 – Part 3   **Cambridge C2 Proficiency: Speaking**

Media Influence – continued

Interlocutor Now, to finish the test, we're going to talk about 'media influence' in general.

Address a selection of the following questions to both candidates:

- What should schools teach young people about media? (Why?)
- Many public figures now receive media training before doing interviews. What do you think about that?
- Do you agree that the media and celebrities depend on each other? (Why / Why not?)
- Are there any stories which the media should be prohibited from reporting? (Why / Why not?)
- Some people are concerned that citizen-led media is devaluing professional journalism. What do you think? (Why?)
- What ethical principles should the field of journalism follow? (Why?)

Interlocutor Thank you. That is the end of the test.

Mark sheet

Date | DD | MM | YY |

Candidate _____

Marks available

Grammatical Resource	0	1	1.5	2	2.5	3	3.5	4	4.5	5
Lexical Resource	0	1	1.5	2	2.5	3	3.5	4	4.5	5
Discourse Management	0	1	1.5	2	2.5	3	3.5	4	4.5	5
Pronunciation	0	1	1.5	2	2.5	3	3.5	4	4.5	5
Interactive Communication	0	1	1.5	2	2.5	3	3.5	4	4.5	5
Global Achievement	0	1	1.5	2	2.5	3	3.5	4	4.5	5

Item descriptors

Grammatical Resource *Control* *Range*	• Degree of control of grammatical forms. • Range of grammatical forms used.
Lexical Resource *Range* *Appropriacy*	• Range of vocabulary used to give and exchange views. • Appropriacy of vocabulary used.
Discourse Management *Extent* *Relevance* *Coherence* *Cohesion*	• Stretches of language produced. • Relevance of contributions and organisation of ideas. • Use of appropriate cohesive devices and discourse markers.
Pronunciation *Intonation* *Stress* *Individual sounds*	• Intelligibility • Intonation • Word stress • Individual sounds
Interactive Communication *Initiating* *Responding* *Development*	• Initiating, responding and linking contributions to other speakers' interventions. • Maintaining and developing interaction, and negotiating towards an outcome. • Widening the scope of the interaction.

Cambridge C2 Proficiency Speaking

Test 6

Test 6 – Part 1	Cambridge C2 Proficiency: Speaking
2 minutes (3 minutes for groups of three)	

Candidates' background

Interlocutor Good morning/afternoon/evening. My name is …………… and this is my colleague …………… .

And your names are?

Could I have your mark sheets, please?

Thank you.

First of all, we'd like to know something about you.

- **Where are you from** *(Candidate A)*? **And you** *(Candidate B)*?
- *[Address Candidate B]* **Are you working or studying at the moment?**
- *[Address Candidate A]* **And you?**

Select a further question for each candidate:

- Can you tell us about the best gift you've ever received?
- What matters most to you when choosing a career or new job? …… (Why?)
- What type of friend are you? …… (Why?)
- What would be your dream home? …… (Why?)
- What aspects of your culture make you feel proud? …… (Why?)
- Would you describe yourself as a decisive person? …… (Why? / Why not?)

Candidates

Interlocutor Thank you.

Cambridge C2 Proficiency: Speaking

Test 6 – Part 2
4 minutes (6 minutes for groups of three)

1 Brochure – careers in sport

Interlocutor Now, in this part of the test you're going to do something together. Here are some pictures of people in different situations.

*Place **Part 2** booklet in front of the candidates. Select **two** of the pictures for the candidates to look at.*

First, I'd like you to look at pictures and talk together about why a career in the sports industry may appeal to many people.

You have about a minute for this, so don't worry if I interrupt you.

Candidates

1 minute (2 minutes for groups of three)

Interlocutor Thank you. Now look at all the pictures.

I'd like you to imagine that a college is putting together a brochure to attract former athletes to apply for a degree. These pictures will be used in the brochure to highlight some of the career paths available to people with a degree.

Talk together about what types of skills are needed to be successful in the careers these pictures show. Then suggest two other careers that former athletes are likely to excel in.

You have about three minutes to talk about this.

Candidates

Approximately 3 minutes (4 minutes for groups of three)

Interlocutor Thank you. (Can I have the booklet, please?) *Retrieve **Part 2** booklet.*

Test 6 – Part 2

1 Brochure – careers in sport

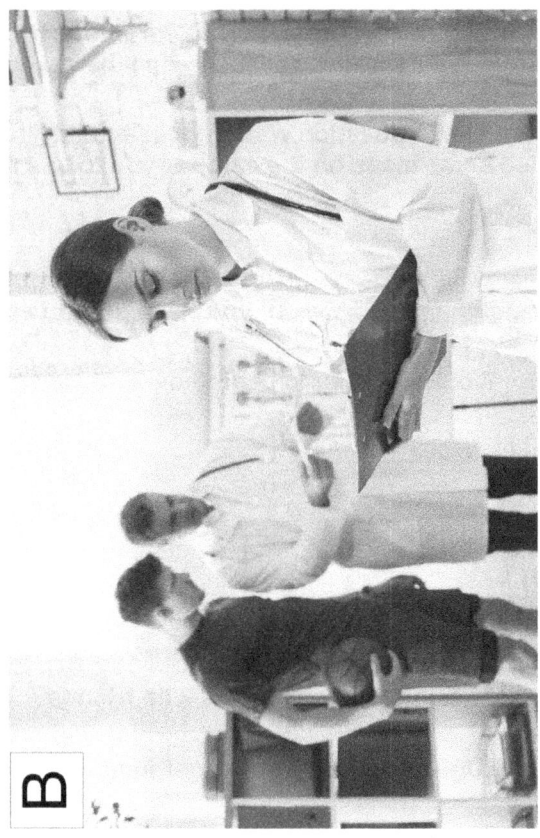
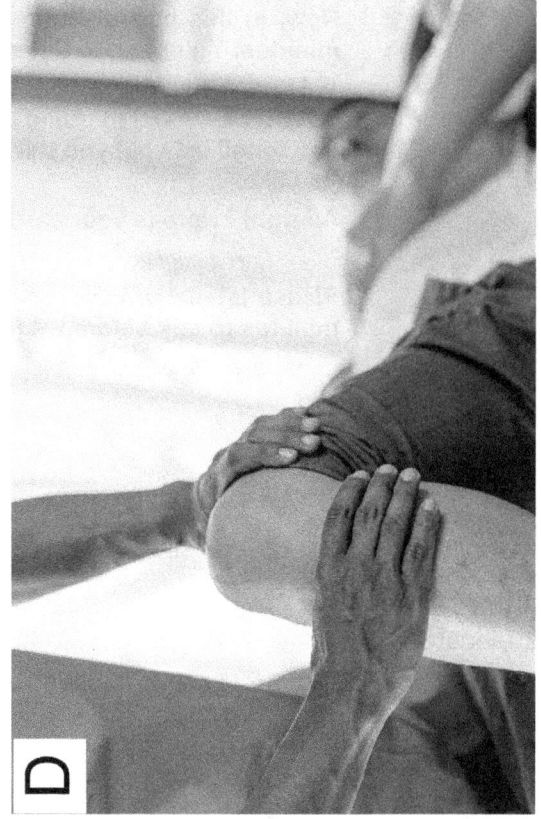

Test 6 – Part 3
Approximately 10 minutes

Cambridge C2 Proficiency: Speaking

Attitudes to Money

Interlocutor	Now, in this part of the test you're each going to talk on your own for about two minutes. You need to listen while your partner is speaking because you'll be asked to comment afterwards.
	So *(Candidate A)*, I'm going to give you a card with a question written on it and I'd like you to tell us what you think. There are also some ideas on the card for you to use if you like.
	All right? Here is your card.
	*Place **Part 3** booklet, open at **Task 1(a)**, in front of Candidate A.*
	Please let *(Candidate B)* **see your card. Remember** *(Candidate A)*, **you have about two minutes to talk before we join in.**
	Allow up to 10 seconds before saying, if necessary: **Would you like to begin now?**
Candidate A	
	2 minutes
Interlocutor	Thank you.
Interlocutor	*Ask **one** of the following questions to Candidate B:*
	• How comfortable do you feel about discussing financial topics with friends? (Why?)
	• Would you say you have a lot of knowledge about managing your finances? (Why? / Why not?)
	• In your country, is it is easy to tell if someone is wealthy? (Why? / Why not?)

> *Invite Candidate A to join in by selecting one of the following prompts:*
> • **What do you think?**
> • **Do you agree?**
> • **How about you?**

Candidates	
	1 minute
Interlocutor	**Thank you. (Can I have the booklet, please?)** *Retrieve **Part 3** booklet.*

Task 1(a)

What can people do to improve their personal finances?

• budgeting

• investing

• consulting an expert

Test 6 – Part 3   Cambridge C2 Proficiency: Speaking

Attitudes to Money – continued

Interlocutor Now *(Candidate B)*, it's your turn to be given a question. Here is your card.

*Place **Part 3** booklet, open at **Task 1(b)**, in front of Candidate B.*

Please let *(Candidate A)* **see your card. Remember** *(Candidate B)*, **you have about two minutes to tell us what you think, and there are some ideas on the card for you to use if you like. All right?**

Allow up to 10 seconds before saying, if necessary: **Would you like to begin now?**

Candidate B

2 minutes

Interlocutor Thank you.

Interlocutor *Ask **one** of the following questions to Candidate A:*
- Would you say that you're generous with your money? (Why? / Why not?)
- Do you feel confident about making important financial decisions? (Why? / Why not?)
- Who has had the greatest influence on your attitudes to money? (Why?)

> *Invite Candidate B to join in by selecting one of the following prompts:*
> - **What do you think?**
> - **Do you agree?**
> - **How about you?**

Candidates

1 minute

Interlocutor Thank you. (Can I have the booklet, please?) *Retrieve **Part 3** booklet.*

Task 1(b)

What can affect people's spending habits?

- access to credit cards
- advertising
- peer pressure

Test 6 – Part 3

Cambridge C2 Proficiency: Speaking

Attitudes to Money – continued

Interlocutor Now, to finish the test, we're going to talk about 'attitudes to money' in general.

Address a selection of the following questions to both candidates:

- It is sometimes said that 'money is the root of all evil'. Do you agree? (Why? / Why not?)
- What would be the potential implications of countries going completely cashless?
- Do you think there should be a limit to how much money an individual should be allowed to have? (Why / Why not?)
- What could be some pitfalls of suddenly coming into a lot of money? (Why?)
- Do you think popular culture celebrates consumerism? (Why? / Why not?)
- In what ways can money affect personal relationships? (Why?)

Interlocutor Thank you. That is the end of the test.

Mark sheet

Date | DD | MM | YY | **Candidate** _____

Marks available

Grammatical Resource	0	1	1.5	2	2.5	3	3.5	4	4.5	5
Lexical Resource	0	1	1.5	2	2.5	3	3.5	4	4.5	5
Discourse Management	0	1	1.5	2	2.5	3	3.5	4	4.5	5
Pronunciation	0	1	1.5	2	2.5	3	3.5	4	4.5	5
Interactive Communication	0	1	1.5	2	2.5	3	3.5	4	4.5	5
Global Achievement	0	1	1.5	2	2.5	3	3.5	4	4.5	5

Item descriptors

Grammatical Resource *Control* *Range*	• Degree of control of grammatical forms. • Range of grammatical forms used.
Lexical Resource *Range* *Appropriacy*	• Range of vocabulary used to give and exchange views. • Appropriacy of vocabulary used.
Discourse Management *Extent* *Relevance* *Coherence* *Cohesion*	• Stretches of language produced. • Relevance of contributions and organisation of ideas. • Use of appropriate cohesive devices and discourse markers.
Pronunciation *Intonation* *Stress* *Individual sounds*	• Intelligibility • Intonation • Word stress • Individual sounds
Interactive Communication *Initiating* *Responding* *Development*	• Initiating, responding and linking contributions to other speakers' interventions. • Maintaining and developing interaction, and negotiating towards an outcome. • Widening the scope of the interaction.

Cambridge C2 Proficiency Speaking

Test 7

Test 7 – Part 1	Cambridge C2 Proficiency: Speaking
2 minutes (3 minutes for groups of three)	

Candidates' background

Interlocutor Good morning/afternoon/evening. My name is .... and this is my colleague ....

And your names are?

Could I have your mark sheets, please?

Thank you.

First of all, we'd like to know something about you.

- **Where are you from** *(Candidate A)*? **And you** *(Candidate B)*?
- *[Address Candidate B]* **Are you working or studying at the moment?**
- *[Address Candidate A]* **And you?**

Select a further question for each candidate:

- Are you more into films or books? ...... (Why?)
- Can you tell us about one of your proudest achievements?
- What activities do you tend to do when you have time off? ...... (Why?)
- What qualities do you look for in a friend? ...... (Why?)
- Would you describe yourself as adventurous? ...... (Why? / Why not?)
- What skill or talent do you wish you had? ...... (Why?)

Candidates

....

Interlocutor Thank you.

Cambridge C2 Proficiency: Speaking

Test 7 – Part 2
4 minutes (6 minutes for groups of three)

1 Report – employee well-being

Interlocutor Now, in this part of the test you're going to do something together. Here are some pictures of people in different situations.

*Place **Part 2** booklet in front of the candidates. Select **two** of the pictures for the candidates to look at.*

First, I'd like you to look at pictures and talk together about how common these situations are in your country.

You have about a minute for this, so don't worry if I interrupt you.

Candidates

1 minute (2 minutes for groups of three)

Interlocutor Thank you. Now look at all the pictures.

I'd like you to imagine that a company is writing a report about how to improve staff well-being. These pictures show some of methods that are being considered.

Talk together about the pros and cons of the activities these pictures show. Then suggest two other things the company should adopt to improve the well-being of its staff.

You have about three minutes to talk about this.

Candidates

Approximately 3 minutes (4 minutes for groups of three)

Interlocutor Thank you. (Can I have the booklet, please?) *Retrieve **Part 2** booklet.*

Test 7 – Part 2
Booklet

Cambridge C2 Proficiency: Speaking

1   Report – employee well-being

Test 7 – Part 3	Cambridge C2 Proficiency: Speaking
Approximately 10 minutes	

The school currirculum

Interlocutor	Now, in this part of the test you're each going to talk on your own for about two minutes. You need to listen while your partner is speaking because you'll be asked to comment afterwards.
	So *(Candidate A)*, I'm going to give you a card with a question written on it and I'd like you to tell us what you think. There are also some ideas on the card for you to use if you like.
	All right? Here is your card.
	*Place **Part 3** booklet, open at **Task 1(a)**, in front of Candidate A.*
	Please let *(Candidate B)* **see your card. Remember** *(Candidate A)*, **you have about two minutes to talk before we join in.**
	Allow up to 10 seconds before saying, if necessary: **Would you like to begin now?**

Candidate A

....

2 minutes

Interlocutor	Thank you.
Interlocutor	*Ask **one** of the following questions to Candidate B:*
	• What age should pupils be allowed to drop subjects they dislike? (Why?)
	• What can schools do to instil an interest in the subjects they teach?
	• Which skills do you wish you'd had the chance to learn at school? (Why?)

> *Invite Candidate A to join in by selecting one of the following prompts:*
> - **What do you think?**
> - **Do you agree?**
> - **How about you?**

Candidates

....

1 minute

Interlocutor	Thank you. (Can I have the booklet, please?) *Retrieve **Part 3** booklet.*

Task 1(a)

Should artistic subjects such as music or drama be compulsory at school?

- **employability**
- **personal growth**
- **connection to academic subjects**

| Test 7 – Part 3 | Cambridge C2 Proficiency: Speaking |

The school curriculum – continued

Interlocutor Now *(Candidate B)*, **it's your turn to be given a question. Here is your card.**

*Place **Part 3** booklet, open at **Task 1(b)**, in front of Candidate B.*

Please let *(Candidate A)* **see your card. Remember** *(Candidate B)*, **you have about two minutes to tell us what you think, and there are some ideas on the card for you to use if you like. All right?**

Allow up to 10 seconds before saying, if necessary: **Would you like to begin now?**

Candidate B

2 minutes

Interlocutor Thank you.

Interlocutor *Ask **one** of the following questions to Candidate A:*
- **Do you think schools offer the right combination of subjects nowadays? (Why? / Why not?)**
- **How involved should parents be in their children's education? (Why?)**
- **Which is more effective: learning academic theories or hands-on practice? (Why?)**

> *Invite Candidate B to join in by selecting one of the following prompts:*
> - **What do you think?**
> - **Do you agree?**
> - **How about you?**

Candidates

1 minute

Interlocutor Thank you. (Can I have the booklet, please?) *Retrieve **Part 3** booklet.*

Task 1(b)

How has school evolved over time?

- **subjects**
- **equipment and resources**
- **teaching methods**

The school curriculum – continued

Interlocutor Now, to finish the test, we're going to talk about 'the school curriculum' in general.

Address a selection of the following questions to both candidates:

- To what extent do people's personal values come from their schooling? (Why?)
- Some people say that schools are too focused on assessment. What do you think?
- Is it realistic to expect schools to prepare students for life? (Why / Why not?)
- In the future, most education will be delivered online. Do you agree? (Why? / Why not?)
- What factors can contribute to the effectiveness of a school? (Why?)
- Why do some governments emphasise the importance of 'lifelong learning'?

Interlocutor Thank you. That is the end of the test.

Mark sheet

| Date | DD | MM | YY | Candidate | _____ |

Marks available

Grammatical Resource	0	1	1.5	2	2.5	3	3.5	4	4.5	5
Lexical Resource	0	1	1.5	2	2.5	3	3.5	4	4.5	5
Discourse Management	0	1	1.5	2	2.5	3	3.5	4	4.5	5
Pronunciation	0	1	1.5	2	2.5	3	3.5	4	4.5	5
Interactive Communication	0	1	1.5	2	2.5	3	3.5	4	4.5	5
Global Achievement	0	1	1.5	2	2.5	3	3.5	4	4.5	5

Item descriptors

Grammatical Resource *Control* *Range*	• Degree of control of grammatical forms. • Range of grammatical forms used.
Lexical Resource *Range* *Appropriacy*	• Range of vocabulary used to give and exchange views. • Appropriacy of vocabulary used.
Discourse Management *Extent* *Relevance* *Coherence* *Cohesion*	• Stretches of language produced. • Relevance of contributions and organisation of ideas. • Use of appropriate cohesive devices and discourse markers.
Pronunciation *Intonation* *Stress* *Individual sounds*	• Intelligibility • Intonation • Word stress • Individual sounds
Interactive Communication *Initiating* *Responding* *Development*	• Initiating, responding and linking contributions to other speakers' interventions. • Maintaining and developing interaction, and negotiating towards an outcome. • Widening the scope of the interaction.

Cambridge C2 Proficiency Speaking

Test 8

Test 8 – Part 1
2 minutes (3 minutes for groups of three)

Cambridge C2 Proficiency: Speaking

Candidates' background

Interlocutor   Good morning/afternoon/evening. My name is …………… and this is my colleague …………… .

And your names are?

Could I have your mark sheets, please?

Thank you.

First of all, we'd like to know something about you.

- **Where are you from** *(Candidate A)*? **And you** *(Candidate B)*?
- *[Address Candidate B]* **Are you working or studying at the moment?**
- *[Address Candidate A]* **And you?**

Select a further question for each candidate:

- Do you think you have enough leisure time? …… (Why? / Why not?)
- Could you tell us about an ambition or future plan you have?
- Do you think (candidate's hometown or region) has changed much in recent years? …… (How? / Why not?)
- What types of food do you typically eat during the week?
- What types of interior design do you find appealing? …… (Why?)
- How important is social media to you? …… (Why?)

Candidates

Interlocutor   Thank you.

Cambridge C2 Proficiency: Speaking

Test 8 – Part 2
4 minutes (6 minutes for groups of three)

1 Report – attracting families to a town

Interlocutor Now, in this part of the test you're going to do something together. Here are some pictures of people in different situations.

*Place **Part 2** booklet in front of the candidates. Select **two** of the pictures for the candidates to look at.*

First, I'd like you to look at pictures and talk together about the potential difficulties people face when moving to a new town.

You have about a minute for this, so don't worry if I interrupt you.

Candidates

1 minute (2 minutes for groups of three)

Interlocutor Thank you. Now look at all the pictures.

I'd like you to imagine that a local authority is putting together a report about how to attract more families to live in its town. These pictures show some of the selling points that families might appreciate.

Talk together about the importance of the points shown in these pictures for families. Then propose two other attractions that could be included in the report.

You have about three minutes to talk about this.

Candidates

Approximately 3 minutes (4 minutes for groups of three)

Interlocutor Thank you. (Can I have the booklet, please?) *Retrieve **Part 2** booklet.*

Cambridge C2 Proficiency: Speaking

Test 8 – Part 2
Booklet

1 Report – attracting families to a town

Test 8 – Part 3	Cambridge C2 Proficiency: Speaking
Approximately 10 minutes	

Health and Well-Being

Interlocutor	**Now, in this part of the test you're each going to talk on your own for about two minutes. You need to listen while your partner is speaking because you'll be asked to comment afterwards.** **So** (Candidate A)**, I'm going to give you a card with a question written on it and I'd like you to tell us what you think. There are also some ideas on the card for you to use if you like.** **All right? Here is your card.** *Place Part 3 booklet, open at Task 1(a), in front of Candidate A.* **Please let** (Candidate B) **see your card. Remember** (Candidate A)**, you have about two minutes to talk before we join in.** *Allow up to 10 seconds before saying, if necessary:* **Would you like to begin now?**
Candidate A	.... *2 minutes*
Interlocutor	**Thank you.**
Interlocutor	*Ask one of the following questions to Candidate B:* • **What would you prioritise to improve your well-being? (Why?)** • **Why might some people feel reluctant to try pampering treatments like massages?** • **Can minor lifestyle changes improve one's well-being? (Why? / Why not?)** *Invite Candidate A to join in by selecting one of the following prompts:* • **What do you think?** • **Do you agree?** • **How about you?**
Candidates	.... *1 minute*
Interlocutor	**Thank you. (Can I have the booklet, please?)** *Retrieve Part 3 booklet.*

Task 1(a)

Is society progressing in the right way when it comes to well-being?

• **healthcare**

• **lifestyle**

• **mental health**

| Test 8 – Part 3 | Cambridge C2 Proficiency: Speaking |

Health and well-being – continued

| Interlocutor | Now *(Candidate B)*, it's your turn to be given a question. Here is your card.

*Place **Part 3** booklet, open at **Task 1(b)**, in front of Candidate B.*

Please let *(Candidate A)* **see your card. Remember** *(Candidate B)*, **you have about two minutes to tell us what you think, and there are some ideas on the card for you to use if you like. All right?**

Allow up to 10 seconds before saying, if necessary: **Would you like to begin now?**

Candidate B

2 minutes

| Interlocutor | Thank you.

| Interlocutor | *Ask **one** of the following questions to Candidate A:*
- **How far do you trust alternative medicine? (Why?)**
- **Where do you get the majority of your health information? (Why?)**
- **How would you change healthcare where you live? (Why?)**

> *Invite Candidate B to join in by selecting one of the following prompts:*
> - **What do you think?**
> - **Do you agree?**
> - **How about you?**

Candidates

1 minute

| Interlocutor | Thank you. (Can I have the booklet, please?) *Retrieve Part 3 booklet.*

Task 1(b)

What factors should be considered when tackling public health issues?

- **culture**
- **education**
- **finances**

Test 8 – Part 3

Cambridge C2 Proficiency: Speaking

Health and well-being – continued

Interlocutor Now, to finish the test, we're going to talk about 'health and well-being' in general.

Address a selection of the following questions to both candidates:

- Do you think leaflets are an effective form of health messaging? (Why? / Why not?)
- What can we learn from older generations about health and well-being?
- How should governments decide which aspects of healthcare to prioritise? (Why?)
- It is sometimes said that the laughter is the best medicine. Do you agree? (Why? / Why not?)
- Should health products be advertised by social media influencers? (Why? / Why not?)
- How can technology improve our well-being?

Interlocutor Thank you. That is the end of the test.

Mark sheet

Date	DD	MM	YY	Candidate	_____

Marks available

Grammatical Resource	0	1	1.5	2	2.5	3	3.5	4	4.5	5
Lexical Resource	0	1	1.5	2	2.5	3	3.5	4	4.5	5
Discourse Management	0	1	1.5	2	2.5	3	3.5	4	4.5	5
Pronunciation	0	1	1.5	2	2.5	3	3.5	4	4.5	5
Interactive Communication	0	1	1.5	2	2.5	3	3.5	4	4.5	5
Global Achievement	0	1	1.5	2	2.5	3	3.5	4	4.5	5

Item descriptors

Grammatical Resource *Control* *Range*	• Degree of control of grammatical forms. • Range of grammatical forms used.
Lexical Resource *Range* *Appropriacy*	• Range of vocabulary used to give and exchange views. • Appropriacy of vocabulary used.
Discourse Management *Extent* *Relevance* *Coherence* *Cohesion*	• Stretches of language produced. • Relevance of contributions and organisation of ideas. • Use of appropriate cohesive devices and discourse markers.
Pronunciation *Intonation* *Stress* *Individual sounds*	• Intelligibility • Intonation • Word stress • Individual sounds
Interactive Communication *Initiating* *Responding* *Development*	• Initiating, responding and linking contributions to other speakers' interventions. • Maintaining and developing interaction, and negotiating towards an outcome. • Widening the scope of the interaction.

Cambridge C2 Proficiency Speaking

Test 9

Test 9 – Part 1
2 minutes (3 minutes for groups of three)

Cambridge C2 Proficiency: Speaking

Candidates' background

Interlocutor Good morning/afternoon/evening. My name is .... and this is my colleague ....

And your names are?

Could I have your mark sheets, please?

Thank you.

First of all, we'd like to know something about you.

- **Where are you from** *(Candidate A)*? **And you** *(Candidate B)*?
- *[Address Candidate B]* **Are you working or studying at the moment?**
- *[Address Candidate A]* **And you?**

Select a further question for each candidate:

- **What things do you generally do to stay healthy?**
- **What sort of people in society do you admire?** ...... **(Why?)**
- **How have your tastes or interests changed as you've got older?** ...... **(Why?)**
- **Can you tell us about a TV show you like or used to like?**
- **How would winning a large sum of money change your daily life?**
- **What sort of research do you do before making large purchases?** ...... **(Why?)**

Candidates

Interlocutor Thank you.

Cambridge C2 Proficiency: Speaking	Test 9 – Part 2
	4 minutes (6 minutes for groups of three)

1   Website – investing one's money

Interlocutor	Now, in this part of the test you're going to do something together. Here are some pictures of different situations.
	*Place **Part 2** booklet in front of the candidates. Select **two** of the pictures for the candidates to look at.*
	First, I'd like you to look at pictures and talk together about the types of factors people consider when investing their money.
	You have about a minute for this, so don't worry if I interrupt you.
Candidates	

1 minute (2 minutes for groups of three)

Interlocutor	Thank you. Now look at all the pictures.
	I'd like you to imagine that a financial website is publishing a blog to show people with little financial expertise some things they can invest a sum of money in. These pictures show some of the investments that are being considered.
	Talk together about the pros and cons of the types of investment shown in these pictures. Then decide which of these investments would stimulate the most amount of interest.
	You have about three minutes to talk about this.
Candidates	

Approximately 3 minutes (4 minutes for groups of three)

Interlocutor	Thank you. (Can I have the booklet, please?) *Retrieve **Part 2** booklet.*

Test 9 – Part 2
Booklet

Cambridge C2 Proficiency: Speaking

1 Website – investing one's money

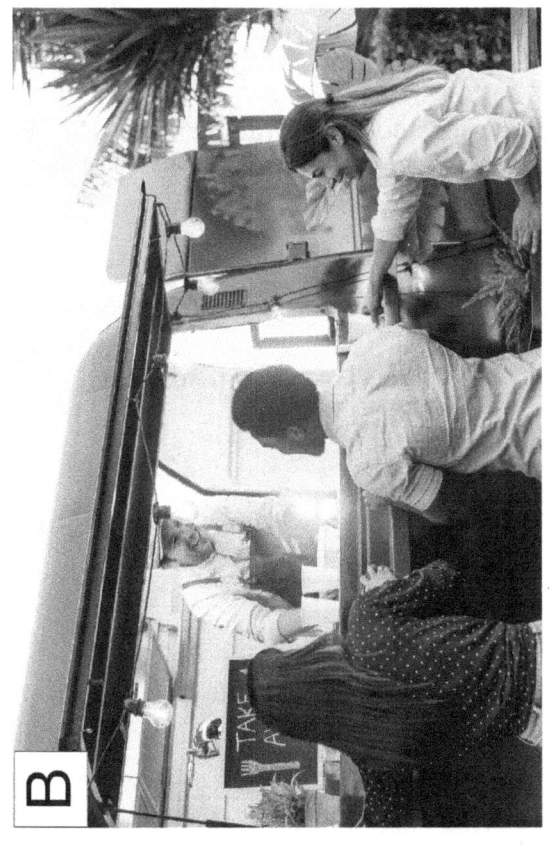

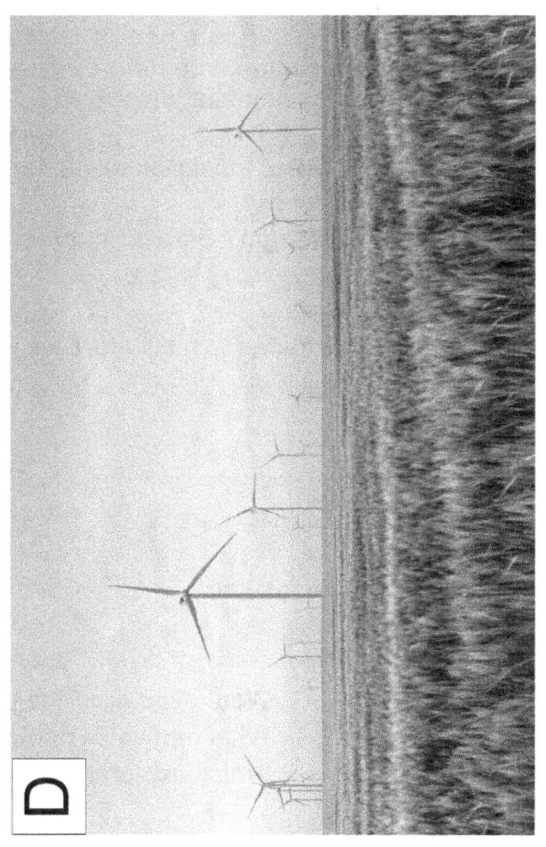

Test 9 – Part 3
Approximately 10 minutes

Cambridge C2 Proficiency: Speaking

Exploration

Interlocutor Now, in this part of the test you're each going to talk on your own for about two minutes. You need to listen while your partner is speaking because you'll be asked to comment afterwards.

So *(Candidate A)*, I'm going to give you a card with a question written on it and I'd like you to tell us what you think. There are also some ideas on the card for you to use if you like.

All right? Here is your card.

*Place **Part 3** booklet, open at **Task 1(a)**, in front of Candidate A.*

Please let *(Candidate B)* see your card. Remember *(Candidate A)*, you have about two minutes to talk before we join in.

Allow up to 10 seconds before saying, if necessary: Would you like to begin now?

Candidate A

....

2 minutes

Interlocutor Thank you.

Interlocutor *Ask **one** of the following questions to Candidate B:*
- Would you describe yourself as a curious person? (Why? / Why not?)
- What motivates people to travel into the unknown?
- Which explorer from history do you admire the most? (Why?)

> *Invite Candidate A to join in by selecting one of the following prompts:*
> - What do you think?
> - Do you agree?
> - How about you?

Candidates

....

1 minute

Interlocutor Thank you. (Can I have the booklet, please?) *Retrieve **Part 3** booklet.*

Task 1(a)

How has exploration shaped the modern world?

- diet
- trade
- science

| Test 9 – Part 3 | Cambridge C2 Proficiency: Speaking |

Exploration – continued

Interlocutor Now *(Candidate B)*, **it's your turn to be given a question. Here is your card.**

*Place **Part 3** booklet, open at **Task 1(b)**, in front of Candidate B.*

Please let *(Candidate A)* **see your card. Remember** *(Candidate B)*, **you have about two minutes to tell us what you think, and there are some ideas on the card for you to use if you like. All right?**

Allow up to 10 seconds before saying, if necessary: **Would you like to begin now?**

Candidate B

2 minutes

Interlocutor Thank you.

Interlocutor *Ask **one** of the following questions to Candidate A:*
- What quality traits make good explorers? (Why? / Why not?)
- What type of exploration interests you the most? (Why?)
- If you could interview an astronaut, what would you ask them? (Why?)

> *Invite Candidate B to join in by selecting one of the following prompts:*
> - **What do you think?**
> - **Do you agree?**
> - **How about you?**

Candidates

1 minute

Interlocutor Thank you. **(Can I have the booklet, please?)** *Retrieve **Part 3** booklet.*

Task 1(b)

What benefits may space exploration bring society?

- **scientific research**
- **resources**
- **international cooperation**

| Test 9 – Part 3 | Cambridge C2 Proficiency: Speaking |

Exploration – continued

Interlocutor Now, to finish the test, we're going to talk about 'exploration' in general.

Address a selection of the following questions to both candidates:

- Which was riskier: sailing to unmapped parts of the world or going into space for the first time? (Why?)
- What should scientists do if they discovered signs of alien life on other planets? (Why?)
- In general, do you think female explorers get enough recognition? (Why / Why not?)
- Do you think exploration leads to conflict or friendship between nations? (Why?)
- How far do inventors and explorers have the same mindset? (Why?)
- What are the ethical implications of space exploration?

Interlocutor Thank you. That is the end of the test.

Mark sheet

Date | DD | MM | YY

Candidate _____

Marks available

Grammatical Resource	0	1	1.5	2	2.5	3	3.5	4	4.5	5
Lexical Resource	0	1	1.5	2	2.5	3	3.5	4	4.5	5
Discourse Management	0	1	1.5	2	2.5	3	3.5	4	4.5	5
Pronunciation	0	1	1.5	2	2.5	3	3.5	4	4.5	5
Interactive Communication	0	1	1.5	2	2.5	3	3.5	4	4.5	5
Global Achievement	0	1	1.5	2	2.5	3	3.5	4	4.5	5

Item descriptors

Grammatical Resource *Control* *Range*	• Degree of control of grammatical forms. • Range of grammatical forms used.
Lexical Resource *Range* *Appropriacy*	• Range of vocabulary used to give and exchange views. • Appropriacy of vocabulary used.
Discourse Management *Extent* *Relevance* *Coherence* *Cohesion*	• Stretches of language produced. • Relevance of contributions and organisation of ideas. • Use of appropriate cohesive devices and discourse markers.
Pronunciation *Intonation* *Stress* *Individual sounds*	• Intelligibility • Intonation • Word stress • Individual sounds
Interactive Communication *Initiating* *Responding* *Development*	• Initiating, responding and linking contributions to other speakers' interventions. • Maintaining and developing interaction, and negotiating towards an outcome. • Widening the scope of the interaction.

Cambridge C2 Proficiency Speaking

Test 10

Test 10 – Part 1	Cambridge C2 Proficiency: Speaking

2 minutes (3 minutes for groups of three)

Candidates' background

Interlocutor Good morning/afternoon/evening. My name is ………….. and this is my colleague ……………. .

And your names are?

Could I have your mark sheets, please?

Thank you.

First of all, we'd like to know something about you.

- **Where are you from** *(Candidate A)*? **And you** *(Candidate B)*?
- *[Address Candidate B]* **Are you working or studying at the moment?**
- *[Address Candidate A]* **And you?**

Select a further question for each candidate:

- **What have you been doing recently?**
- **Do you tend to plan things carefully or act on impulse?** …… **(Why?)**
- **How important is spending time in nature to you?** …… **(Why?)**
- **Do you use public transport very often where you live?** …… **(Why? / Why not?)**
- **Do you prefer learning practical skills or studying academic subjects?** …… **(Why?)**
- **Can you tell us about a cultural tradition that's important to you?**

Candidates

Interlocutor Thank you.

Cambridge C2 Proficiency: Speaking

Test 10 – Part 2
4 minutes (6 minutes for groups of three)

1 Article – studying abroad

Interlocutor Now, in this part of the test you're going to do something together. Here are some pictures of people in different situations.

*Place **Part 2** booklet in front of the candidates. Select **two** of the pictures for the candidates to look at.*

First, I'd like you to look at pictures and talk together about how the people might be feeling in these situations.

You have about a minute for this, so don't worry if I interrupt you.

Candidates

1 minute (2 minutes for groups of three)

Interlocutor Thank you. Now look at all the pictures.

I'd like you to imagine that a magazine is planning an article giving advice to students who are thinking of studying abroad. These pictures will be used in the article to show some of the situations international students may encounter.

Talk together about what colleges can do to address the issues shown in the pictures. Then decide which of these pictures should <u>not</u> be used in the article.

You have about three minutes to talk about this.

Candidates

Approximately 3 minutes (4 minutes for groups of three)

Interlocutor Thank you. (Can I have the booklet, please?) *Retrieve **Part 2** booklet.*

Test 10 – Part 2
Booklet

Cambridge C2 Proficiency: Speaking

1 Article – studying abroad

Test 10 – Part 3	Cambridge C2 Proficiency: Speaking
Approximately 10 minutes	

The influence of groups

Interlocutor — Now, in this part of the test you're each going to talk on your own for about two minutes. You need to listen while your partner is speaking because you'll be asked to comment afterwards.

So *(Candidate A)*, I'm going to give you a card with a question written on it and I'd like you to tell us what you think. There are also some ideas on the card for you to use if you like.

All right? Here is your card.

*Place **Part 3** booklet, open at **Task 1(a)**, in front of Candidate A.*

Please let *(Candidate B)* see your card. Remember *(Candidate A)*, you have about two minutes to talk before we join in.

Allow up to 10 seconds before saying, if necessary: **Would you like to begin now?**

Candidate A

....
2 minutes

Interlocutor — Thank you.

Interlocutor — *Ask **one** of the following questions to Candidate B:*
- What role do you typically take when in a group situation? (Why?)
- What skills can help group projects work more smoothly?
- Do you think working in a group is more time-efficient? (Why? / Why not?)

> *Invite Candidate A to join in by selecting one of the following prompts:*
> - What do you think?
> - Do you agree?
> - How about you?

Candidates

....
1 minute

Interlocutor — Thank you. (Can I have the booklet, please?) *Retrieve **Part 3** booklet.*

Task 1(a)

Why are group projects a common form of assessment in higher education?

• collaborative learning

• practicality

• authenticity

| Test 10 – Part 3 | Cambridge C2 Proficiency: Speaking |

The influence of groups – continued

| Interlocutor | Now *(Candidate B)*, it's your turn to be given a question. Here is your card.

*Place **Part 3** booklet, open at **Task 1(b)**, in front of Candidate B.*

Please let *(Candidate A)* **see your card. Remember** *(Candidate B)*, **you have about two minutes to tell us what you think, and there are some ideas on the card for you to use if you like. All right?**

Allow up to 10 seconds before saying, if necessary: **Would you like to begin now?**

Candidate B

....
2 minutes

| Interlocutor | Thank you.

| Interlocutor | *Ask **one** of the following questions to Candidate A:*
- **What type of online campaigns attract your attention? (Why?)**
- **Do you think online surveys give companies reliable information? (Why? / Why not?)**
- **Would you describe yourself as a team player? (Why? / Why not?)**

> *Invite Candidate B to join in by selecting one of the following prompts:*
> - **What do you think?**
> - **Do you agree?**
> - **How about you?**

Candidates

....
1 minute

| Interlocutor | Thank you. (Can I have the booklet, please?) *Retrieve **Part 3** booklet.*

Task 1(b)

How has technology increased the power of groups?

- politics
- charity
- research

Test 10 – Part 3

Cambridge C2 Proficiency: Speaking

The influence of groups – continued

Interlocutor — Now, to finish the test, we're going to talk about 'the influence of groups' in general.

Address a selection of the following questions to both candidates:

- Do you think most societies value individuality or conformity more? (Why?)
- What can prevent group members from working effectively together?
- To what extent is diversity an advantage in groups? (Why?)
- It is sometimes said that a team can be greater than the sum of its parts. What do you think about this? (Why?)
- Do you think political success comes more from collaboration or individual leadership? (Why?)
- In what ways have groups changed society?

Interlocutor — Thank you. That is the end of the test.

Mark sheet

Date	DD	MM	YY		Candidate	_____

Marks available

Grammatical Resource	0	1	1.5	2	2.5	3	3.5	4	4.5	5
Lexical Resource	0	1	1.5	2	2.5	3	3.5	4	4.5	5
Discourse Management	0	1	1.5	2	2.5	3	3.5	4	4.5	5
Pronunciation	0	1	1.5	2	2.5	3	3.5	4	4.5	5
Interactive Communication	0	1	1.5	2	2.5	3	3.5	4	4.5	5
Global Achievement	0	1	1.5	2	2.5	3	3.5	4	4.5	5

Item descriptors

Grammatical Resource *Control* *Range*	• Degree of control of grammatical forms. • Range of grammatical forms used.
Lexical Resource *Range* *Appropriacy*	• Range of vocabulary used to give and exchange views. • Appropriacy of vocabulary used.
Discourse Management *Extent* *Relevance* *Coherence* *Cohesion*	• Stretches of language produced. • Relevance of contributions and organisation of ideas. • Use of appropriate cohesive devices and discourse markers.
Pronunciation *Intonation* *Stress* *Individual sounds*	• Intelligibility • Intonation • Word stress • Individual sounds
Interactive Communication *Initiating* *Responding* *Development*	• Initiating, responding and linking contributions to other speakers' interventions. • Maintaining and developing interaction, and negotiating towards an outcome. • Widening the scope of the interaction.

Model answers

Test 1

Speaking CPE

Model answers – Test 1

The C2 Proficiency examination is usually taken by candidates who want to obtain a C2-level certificate, which generally corresponds to a native-like level of English. As described by the Common European Framework of Reference for Languages (CEFRL), candidates with a C1 level are considered to be *proficient users*, that is, users who show *mastery* or *comprehensive operational proficiency* of the English language, thus being able to:

- understand with ease virtually everything heard or read

- summarise information from different spoken and written sources, reconstructing arguments and accounts in a coherent presentation

- express themselves spontaneously, fluently and precisely, discerning finer shades of meaning even in more complex situations.

The purpose of the following model answers is to provide teachers and candidates with an example of language production and test performance that would score a high mark in a real C2 Proficiency Speaking test.

These answers contain grammatical and lexical features as well as a range of discourse resources suited to an advanced level of English.

Please note that great linguistic accuracy is expected at C2 level.

On pages 115–120, there are comments highlighting different aspects of the model answers, such as:

- the strategies candidates make use of to address some of the parts

- the ways in which candidates express their opinions

- how candidates interact with one another, etc.

The aim of these comments is to draw the reader's attention to important details that might help them to achieve a successful performance in this part of the C2 Proficiency examination.

While reading the model answers and the examiner's comments, please bear in mind the following:

- The test is taken in pairs (or trios), and candidates are expected to interact with each other.

- The approximate timing of each part of the test is as follows:

    o Part 1: 2 minutes (pair) / 3 minutes (trio)

    o Part 2: 4 minutes (pair) / 6 minutes (trio)

    o Part 3: 10 minutes (pair) / 15 minutes (trio)

- These model answers would achieve a high score in a C2 Proficiency Speaking test, and so should be regarded as strong-performance answers that provide examples of the types of linguistic structures candidates are expected to produce at this level rather than examples of minimum performance to pass.

Model answers

Test 1 – Part 1 – Model answers

Interlocutor	Where are you from, Candidate A?
Candidate A	*I'm from Andalucía, a region in the south of Spain.*
Interlocutor	And you, Candidate B?
Candidate B	*Likewise, I'm also from Spain, but from a small town just to the north of Barcelona.*
Interlocutor	Are you working or studying at the moment?
Candidate B	*Well, I'm currently doing an internship at an accountancy firm in Seville, you know, as part of my degree.*
Interlocutor	And you?
Candidate A	*To be honest, as I've just graduated, I haven't really started my job hunt yet. But all being well, I think I can secure a post at an engineering firm before long.*
Interlocutor	What activities do you find relaxing?
Candidate A	*Well, I suppose it's a bit of a cliché but you can't beat a day at the beach. Swimming and a spot of sunbathing are all I need to unwind and recharge my batteries. All the better when I'm hanging out with friends at the same time.*
Interlocutor	Would you describe yourself as creative?
Candidate B	*Not really in the sense of drawing or painting or anything like that. But I'd class myself as a creative thinker. After all, my field, engineering, is all about finding novel solutions and to do that, you really do need to have the mindset of a disruptor, meaning looking at things from different perspectives. And I'm also good at thinking on my feet!*
Interlocutor	Thank you.

Test 1 – Part 2 – Model answers

Report – Mass tourism

Task 1 – Short discussion

Interlocutor	First, I'd like you to look at pictures B and C, and talk together about the potential impacts of mass tourism on local communities. You have about a minute for this, so don't worry if I interrupt you.
Candidate A	*Would you like to kick off?*
Candidate B	*Sure. Let's see… Well, I think we can both agree that these situations are fairly common scenarios, especially the way you can feel packed in like sardines when you're visiting a popular area – just look at picture B! If you happen to live in an area like that, peak season must feel terribly suffocating when you're just trying to go about your business. What's your take?*
Candidate A	*Well, yes, as you say, having so many visitors descend on your town or village can be a lot to contend with, especially if the local infrastructure isn't up to the challenge. Actually, I'd argue that's the real issue, which I suppose brings us to picture C, with the diggers and trucks. Because, well, where tourism starts, inevitably construction and development follow. But you've got to wonder whether that's necessarily something to be desired.*
Candidate B	*Indeed, I mean, quite apart from all the obvious upheaval and disruption for residents, you also need to look at the bigger picture. See, in this image, they're obviously in the process of developing an area, maybe they're going to build a hotel complex or something. But at what cost? As far as I'm concerned, overdevelopment can completely ruin the natural charm of a place. It*

Speaking CPE

	looks like they're having to get rid of a lot of greenery for whatever it is they're building. What do you think?
Candidate A	Ah, yeah, I'm with you on that one. And that's before you even go into the environmental consequences. But I suppose an influx of tourists does present economic opportunities too.
Interlocutor	Thank you. Now look at all the pictures.

Test 1 – Part 2 (continued) – Model answers

Task 2 – Long discussion

Interlocutor	I'd like you to imagine that a committee is writing a report about the pros and cons of bringing mass tourism to the local area. These pictures will be used to show some of the problems associated with mass tourism.
	Talk together about what can be done locally to address the issues that these pictures show. Then decide which of these issues should be the main focus of the committee's report. You have about three minutes to talk about this.
Candidate A	Shall I go first now?
Candidate B	Of course, go ahead.
Candidate A	Well, it strikes me that the issue of overcrowding is about controlling the speed with which tourist areas develop. And of course, tourists have their part to play by choosing to go off the beaten track more or visiting places in low season, so I'm not sure that's the right one to focus on. What do you think?
Candidate B	I see what you mean, and actually, sustainability is the issue that's at the forefront of most people's minds now, so that seems like the most logical place to start. I mean, we've already touched on it – overdevelopment can be disastrous for the environment, can't it?
Candidate A	Yes, absolutely, and for me, the image that resonates with me the most is the one with all the rubbish on the beach. I can't think of a starker image to highlight the potential impacts of uncontrolled mass tourism. On the one hand, you've got the shoreline and a lovely looking beach which is what a lot of people associate with tourism, but at the same time, look at all that waste. And we all know what that can do to our waterways and wildlife.
Candidate B	Couldn't agree more. It's clearly something the local council should get to grips with if they're serious about attracting more tourists to the area. I mean, surely that wouldn't be so hard to tackle? Wouldn't you agree?
Candidate A	For sure. And the good news is people are becoming increasingly willing to recycle their waste or dispose of it responsibly. And of course, some authorities that issue on-the-spot fines for littering. But even so, waste management presents huge challenges in tourist areas.
Candidate B	Well, talking of challenges, I'd imagine all the transportation implications would have an even greater impact on the local area. That image of gridlocked traffic sums it up pretty well, doesn't it? That's what I had in mind when I was thinking about sustainability. Just think of the carbon emissions of all those vehicles, and how air quality will suffer.
Candidate A	Well, that's a good point, come to think of it. And excuse the pun, but there are several ways to navigate this issue. I mean, obviously implementing traffic-calming schemes or even banning vehicles from town centres is one approach, but it's bound to have knock-on effects elsewhere. At least, that's been the case in my hometown where parking has become a nightmare in the residential suburbs.
Candidate B	Yes, we're in the same boat where I live too. So, do you think there are better alternatives? Public transport perhaps?

Candidate A	*Well, yes, investing in options like trams or buses has got to come into the equation. Even better, having a comprehensive cycle network is something that can alleviate traffic congestion, and actually enhances the quality of life for everyone. So I think you've hit the nail on the head – this is the issue that should be the priority for the council in the report. And I don't know about you, but the transport options are something I consider when I'm deciding where to go on holiday.*
Candidate B	*Oh, yeah, I'm the same. I'll always plump for somewhere that has convenient transport connections. So are we in agreement? The main issue should be to address the potential traffic congestion that mass tourism can bring.*
Candidate A	*Yep, I think so. I mean, that's not to downplay all the other problems that we can see in these images. But I do think it's the most complex one, whereas the issue of construction and its impact on the environment is relatively simple to control. That's basically about putting laws or regulations in place to ensure any construction is undertaken in a responsible way.*
Candidate B	*Yeah, you're dead right, although it's a pity that many resorts put business ahead of environmental concerns.*
Interlocutor	Thank you.

Test 1 – Part 3 – Model answers

Leadership

Task 1 – Long turn

Card A	What qualities make an effective leader? • communication • vision • decision making

Candidate A	*Let's see...*
	Well, let me start by saying that, in my humble opinion, I'm not convinced we can talk about a 'one-size-fits-all' approach to leadership because what might be lauded as decisive in one context might be viewed as overbearing or stubborn in another.
	But having said that, whether it be business, sports or the military, I can't think of a single situation where communication doesn't play a part. It's such an integral part of working with others, especially if you're in a leadership role. Leaders who communicate their expectations clearly command respect of course, but even more importantly, they're able to motivate their team, which improves morale and in turn leads to better outcomes. Similarly, effective communication can help leaders when things go wrong. What I mean is that there will always be internal conflicts or disputes for leaders to smooth over, so they have to be diplomatic and also identify the best way to reason with people. Personally speaking, I think I'd find that quite a challenge.
	Other than that, I suppose another thing that leaders should strive for is vision. Unless you've got a clear idea of what you want to achieve, then you're not going to get very far. But that doesn't mean that a leader should be closed off to input from other people, quite the opposite in fact. The way I see it, the leader should have a general sense of where the team should be going, but should be able to collaborate with others about how to get there. It really boils down to the leader having the bigger picture rather than micromanaging or obsessing about finer details. And of course, this vision will help them take the key decisions, which is the aspect I'd like to discuss now.
	I do think there's a fine line between being collaborative and respecting other people's views and being indecisive. Effective leaders realise that ultimately, the buck stops with them, meaning they're the ones who have the final say. So, being able to evaluate often contradictory or confusing

	information is crucial. They need to be able understand how different scenarios are likely to play out and also, be responsive in dynamic situations.
Interlocutor	Thank you. Candidate B, what difficulties can arise when making the transition from team member to team leader?
Candidate B	*Erm, yeah, that must be a tricky situation. I'd imagine the leader may feel like they have to over-compensate and go out of their way to be friendly and approachable just so it doesn't look like they've become arrogant. But then of course, the risk is that they become too lenient. Or maybe it can go the opposite way, with the team leader desperate to exert their new authority by throwing their weight around. That's obviously going to alienate everyone, isn't it?*
Interlocutor	Do you agree?
Candidate A	*Well, yes, I can definitely imagine both of those situations. And maybe another difficulty might be a team members feelings being put out because someone has been promoted ahead of them. That could cause tensions or resentment.*
Interlocutor	Thank you.

Card B	Why does leadership appeal to some people? • status • making a difference • autonomy

Candidate B	*Alright, so I'll be talking about why leadership seems to appeal to some people, and of course, it's hard to generalise. But I'll discuss what I perceive to be some of the selling points of taking on a leadership role.*
	Firstly, let's start with a reason that might be a little contentious, but it's something we can't really ignore… how can I put this? Well, um, basically, many people like the power or status that they think leadership gives them. Who wouldn't want to be respected or seen as the person at the top? And that's before you get into all the material benefits such as a better salary or whatever. And I'd even go as far as to say that wanting power is more of a driver for many high-profile politicians than anything else. I don't know if that makes them attention seekers or whether there's been any academic research into the personality traits of leaders, but I can't imagine anyone actively seeking out such roles as being shy or modest types.
	And erm… that sort of goes hand in hand with another reason leadership might appeal to people. I suspect people might crave the autonomy of a leadership role. Either they prefer to strike out on their own, maybe as an entrepreneur or something like that, or they feel that they're well placed to make difficult decisions. A lot of people thrive on the cut and thrust of leadership roles and relish the responsibility that comes with being a leader. And let's be honest, these people simply don't want to blend in. They want to do things their way. Nothing wrong with that of course, but anyone who thinks they can do it all alone is probably quite naïve.
	Now, let me move on to my final point, and it's one that puts more of a positive slant on things. I'd like to think that external benefits such as power or status are only a small part of the story, and that for most leaders in most walks of life there's an underlying desire to make a difference. I mean, working as part of a group can be incredibly rewarding, but there are inevitable compromises that have to be made or instances where you might feel constrained by the parameters within which you're working. So anyone with strong convictions, you know, like a burning desire to achieve something – maybe a vision, to go back to what was said before – might feel that being a leader will give them a greater chance of making their mark. And that's particularly true when it comes to people who really want to bring about radical change. I'd put people like environmental campaigners or pioneering feminists in this category. I'm sure we can think of other individuals, too…

Model answers

Test 1 – Part 3 (continued) – Model answers

Interlocutor	Thank you. Candidate A, to what extent do leaders have to be ruthless?
Candidate A	*Well, um… it depends. They definitely have to be willing to make unpopular decisions if that's in the best interests of their team, or company, or whatever. But still, providing it's done for principled reasons, I think that's acceptable. If you mean ruthless in the sense of doing whatever it takes to win at all costs, then no. You have to draw the line somewhere.*
Interlocutor	Do you agree?
Candidate B	*Yes, I do, or at least, I'd certainly hope that leaders can get to the top without being unscrupulous. But maybe it depends on the industry you're in. There's one field that's notoriously ruthless, which is elite sports management, especially football. The top clubs hire and fire managers all the time.*
Interlocutor	Thank you.

Task 2 – Question-based discussion

Interlocutor	Do you think leaders are born or made?
Candidate A	*Oh, they're made, surely. No doubt some people gravitate towards leadership more naturally than others, but it's all about your environment. If you've been exposed to opportunities to take on leadership, it'll be something that you feel comfortable with. That's why it's important to encourage students to develop leadership skills. At least, that's my view. How do you see it?*
Candidate B	*Honestly, I couldn't have put it better myself. And to pick up on your point about education, I'd say that parents have a role to play too. If they give children responsibility and a certain degree of independence at an early age, that's likely to help them develop leadership skills.*
Interlocutor	Candidate B, some people say that role models and leaders are different things. What do you think?
Candidate B	*Erm… I've never really thought about that before. But I'd say that maybe a leader simply describes what a person does, whether positive or negative. So, that could be the captain of a sports team, a manager or a president. But a role model has positive connotations. It's someone you admire and want to emulate. In an ideal world, there would be plenty of overlap between the two, course.*
Interlocutor	Do you agree, Candidate A?
Candidate A	*I do, yes. And it makes me wonder whether the best leaders are the ones who actually set out to lead by example, you know, so they're actually serving as role models.*
Interlocutor	In general, do you think leaders get enough respect in society?
Candidate A	*Well, we've been talking about power and status, which could be construed as respect, couldn't it? So, in a way, there's this perception that leaders are the ones who have the greatest respect in society. But at the same time, I think they're also the ones who come under the closest scrutiny, although you might see it differently, Candidate B!*
Candidate B	*I was going to say the same thing, actually. And maybe the media, at least in some countries, take great delight in bringing them down. So we put leaders on a pedestal and then we end up disappointed when they don't meet our unrealistic expectations.*
Interlocutor	It is sometimes said that the most effective leaders are invisible. Do you agree?

Test 1 – Part 3 (continued) – Model answers

Candidate B *Wow, that's a tough one, to be honest. Erm… I'm not sure what that could mean. Does it mean they don't do much? Or that their actions have little impact? Well, that doesn't make sense because the leaders obviously do make a difference. So I'd have to disagree because leaders are the driving force by definition. What's your opinion?*

Candidate A *Ah, well I'd interpret the saying differently. To me, what it's driving at is the idea that leaders tend to have more success when they let other people shine. They don't have to get the limelight all the time to drive their ideas forward. And there's probably some truth in that.*

Interlocutor Is being popular a must for leaders? (Why? / Why not?)

Candidate B *Well, it certainly doesn't hurt. I mean, they need to have the support from their team if they want to implement difficult policies, don't they?*

Candidate A *No doubt, yes. But at the same time, they shouldn't let other people's perceptions of them stop them from doing what they feel is right.*

Interlocutor How useful is it for leaders to have an understanding of psychology?

Candidate A *As far as I'm concerned, it's essential. I mean, leaders presumably spend a large portion of their time trying to figure out what makes people tick in order to identify what will persuade them to do certain things. Would you agree with me, Candidate B?*

Candidate B *I agree, but only up to a certain point. I don't think you're implying that leaders should use psychology to manipulate or trick people, are you? Because that's not the way I see it. But yes, understanding psychology can help leaders find ways to get the best out of their team. And it can also be useful as a tool for self-reflection and introspection too, of course.*

Interlocutor Thank you. That is the end of the test.

Examiner comments

Test 1

Speaking CPE

Examiner comments

Test 1 – Part 1 – Model answers

In Part 1, candidates are asked about themselves, their background and experiences.

These questions are scripted, and the interlocutor will never improvise them. Candidates are expected to answer and justify their responses, but these should not turn into a long monologue. If the answer given to a question is particularly short, the examiner will probably ask a follow-up question such as "Why?" or "Why not?". Therefore, candidates should answer more than a simple "Yes", "No" or one-word answer, but not much more.

For example:

Question	Are you working or studying at the moment?
Answer	Well, as I've just graduated, I haven't really started my job hunt yet. But all being well, I think I can secure a post at an engineering firm before long.

Given the nature of the conversation, these answers should sound natural and non-rehearsed. Sounding natural is part of being fluent in a language, so using some informal expressions (*pretty sure*), exclamations (*Fingers crossed!*), contractions (*I'm, don't*) or discourse markers *(Well)* is actually encouraged, as long as they are natural and not used excessively.

As this is a C2-level speaking test, candidates' answers should show C2-level grammar and vocabulary, even in Part 1, if possible. For this reason, in the model answers provided for Part 1, there are some appropriate-level phrases like:

- *all being well*
- *secure a post*
- *it's a bit of a cliché but…*
- *can't beat*
- *a spot of…*
- *unwind and recharge my batteries*
- *all the better*
- *have the mindset*
- *thinking on my feet*
- *etc.*

Part 1 is probably not the most suitable part for candidates to prove their level, but they should still try to show what they know, and, above all, try to sound natural.

Key things to practise:

- Talking about personal background referring to past, present and future situations
- Providing brief examples to illustrate points (e.g. *as was the case when I was at university*)
- Using a range of phrases to respond to "yes/no" questions (e.g. *Fortunately I do, yes, because…; Not as much as I'd like, sadly…; Maybe in the sense of…*)

Test 1 – Part 2 – Model answers

In Part 2, candidates are expected to work together on two different tasks: an introductory discussion reacting to a maximum of two pictures, and a decision-making task in which various pictures are used. They are supposed to engage in a discussion that should, if possible, culminate in a common decision or suggestion to solve a problem.

Examiner comments

Task 1 – introductory discussion
In this task, candidates respond to one or two pictures. The aim of this task is to familiarise the candidates with the general theme that they will explore in more depth in Task 2. As such, candidates are expected to keep in mind both what they can see in the images and use these images as a springboard to talk about the general theme (e.g. 'effects of mass tourism').

Task 2 – long discussion
This task is somewhat more abstract in nature as it involves the candidates using the entire set of images (i.e. the ones they saw in Task 1, and some additional images) as prompts to help them reach an agreement about a specific question or scenario. Common tasks will require candidates to rank, select or classify. Candidates will also be required to discuss a particular question (e.g. *what can be done locally to address the issues?*)

As this is a C2-level test, candidates' grammar and vocabulary are expected to be excellent and there is special emphasis on assessing their interactive and communicative skills, such as speculating, comparing, providing and eliciting opinions and reactions, evaluating, negotiating and so on.

Notice the following elements in the model answers on pages 107–114:

The language candidates use

If we take a look at Candidate A and Candidate B's comparisons, we notice that they:

- **use appropriate C2 grammar and lexis:** *common scenarios ... packed in like sardines ... terribly suffocating ... go about your business ... descend on ... a lot to contend with ... isn't up to the challenge ... inevitably ... necessarily something to be desired ... quite apart from the obvious upheaval and disruption ... look at the bigger picture ... the natural charm of a place ... an influx of tourists ... controlling the speed with which ... go off the beaten track ... in low season ... at the forefront of most people's minds ... starker image ... waterways ... should get to grips with ... are becoming increasingly willing to ... issue on-the-spot fines ... gridlocked traffic ... carbon emissions ... excuse the pun but ... navigate this issue ... implementing traffic-calming schemes ... bound to have ... knock-on effects elsewhere ... has become a nightmare in the residential suburbs ... come into the equation ... a comprehensive cycle network ... alleviate traffic congestion ... plump for ... putting laws or regulations into place ...*

- **express views and opinions:** *I think ... just look at ... I'd argue that ... you've got to wonder whether ... I mean ... As far as I'm concerned ... but I suppose ... it strikes me that ... I'm not sure that's the right one to focus on ... and for me ... that resonates with me the most ... I can't think of a ... And we all know that ... It's clearly ... I'd imagine that ... sums it up pretty well ... That's what I had in mind when I was thinking about ... Just think of ... I don't know about you but ... but I do think ...*

- **agree and disagree:** *Indeed ... Yeah, I'm with you on that one ... I see what you mean ... Yes, absolutely ... but at the same time... Couldn't agree more ... For sure ... but even so ... Well, that's a good point, come to think of it ... yes, we're in the same boat where I live ... well, yes, investing in options like trams or buses has got to come into the equation ... so I think you've hit the nail on the head ... Oh yeah, I'm the same ... Yep, I think so ... but that's not to downplay ... Yeah, you're dead right ... although it's a pity that ...*

- **employ turn-taking gambits:** *would you like to kick off? ... Sure, let's see ... What's your take? ... What do you think? ... Shall I go first now? ... Of course, go ahead ... can't it? ... Wouldn't you agree? ... Well, talking of challenges ... So, do you think there are better alternatives? Public transport perhaps? ...*

These expressions show that candidates are capable of initiating, responding and linking contributions to each other's turn, and that they can develop a successful interaction and negotiate towards an outcome in a very natural way.

In this case, both candidates reach an agreement by the end. However, this is by no means a test requirement and candidates' marks will not be affected by whether an agreement or conclusion is reached or not.

Finally, it is extremely important that this part does not turn into two separate, individual turns at speaking rather than a seamless interaction. Therefore, candidates should avoid lengthy answers and should try to involve their partner at the end of each turn to keep the conversation flowing.

Key thing to practise:

- Linking to and building on the partner's turn by referring to their ideas (e.g. *Well, as you say, we've already touched on it, talking of ...; going back to what you said about ...*)

Test 1 – Part 3 – Model answers

In Part 3, each candidate is presented with a card with a question and three prompts on it. They then have two minutes to develop a monologue around the topic of their cards. This is a chance for candidates to show how well they can speak on their own in a longer turn.

Candidates' grammar and vocabulary are expected to be excellent and, more specifically in this part, there is special emphasis on their discourse management – i.e. how long they can speak for (*extent*), how relevant their contributions (*relevance*) are and how well they can organise and connect their speech (*coherence* and *cohesion*).

Please note that even though two minutes might seem like a long time, it is common for candidates to be interrupted when the time is up before they have finished. However, this does not mean that it will affect the candidate's mark negatively, as long as what he/she has said has been delivered using C2-level grammar and vocabulary in a well-organised speech.

After each long turn, there are two follow-up questions that give the candidates the chance to react to their partner's opinions. It is extremely important that they both pay attention to the other's monologue so that they can respond to these questions more appropriately.

Finally, the interlocutor leads a guided discussion in which both candidates are asked to answer some questions and react to their partner's answers. These final questions stem from the topic developed as part of the candidates' long turns. These are usually thematically complex questions, and they will have to answer them either individually or as a short discussion with their partner. The main goal of this task is to produce longer stretches of language as part of a conversation in which candidates show their ability to discuss a topic to a more complex extent. It is, therefore, a great opportunity for candidates to provide answers that are organised and insightful, and to make sure that their grammar and lexis are as good as that expected for a C2-level exam.

Now let us go over some important aspects to consider.

The language candidates use

If we take a look at the candidates' model answers, we notice that they:

- **use appropriate C2 grammar and lexis:** *... a 'one-size fits all' approach ... what might be lauded as ... viewed as overbearing or stubborn ... whether it be business, sports or the military ... such an integral part of ... command respect ... improves morale ... which in turn leads to ... there will always be internal conflicts or disputes .... smooth over ... diplomatic ... it really boils down to ... there's a fine line between ... often contradictory or confusing information ... be responsive in dynamic situations ... overcompensate ... go out of their way to ... exert their new authority ... throw their weight* *around ... alienate everyone ... feeling put out ... contentious ... more of a driver ... actively seeking out roles ... strike out on their own ... puts more of a positive slant on things ... constrained by the parameters within which you're working ... strong convictions ... a burning desire to ... making their mark ... you have to draw the line somewhere ... positive connotations ... emulate ... plenty of overlap between the two ... could be construed as ... come under the closest scrutiny ... put leaders on a pedestal ... get the limelight ... what makes people tick ... self-reflection and introspection ...*

- **use cohesive devices and discourse markers to organise their speech:** *let me start by saying ... but having said that ... similarly ... but even more importantly ... other than that ... another thing ... which is the aspect I'd like to discuss now ... I'll be talking about ... but I'll discuss ... firstly, let's start with ... that sort of goes hand in hand with another reason ... now let me move on to my final point, and it's one that ... but at the same time ... well, we've been talking about ...*

- **are capable of expressing complex opinions, eliciting reactions and reacting accordingly:** *in my humble opinion ... I'm not convinced we can ... what I mean is that ... I do think there's a fine line between ... well, yes, I can definitely imagine both of those situations ... might be a little contentious but it's something we can't really ignore ... how can I put this? ... Yes, I do, or at least, I'd certainly hope ... But maybe it depends on the industry you're in ... Oh, they're made, surely ... At least, that's my view ... how do you see it? ... Honestly, I couldn't have put it better myself ... erm ... I've never really thought about that before ... but I'd say ... So I'd have to disagree ... and it makes me wonder whether ... although you might see it differently ... I was going to say the same thing, actually ... what's your opinion? ... well, I'd interpret the saying differently ... to me, what it's getting at is ... there's probably some truth in that ... no doubt, yes ... as far as I'm concerned, it's essential ... would you agree with me? ... I agree, but only up to a certain point ... I don't think you're implying that ... that's not the way I see it ...*

Candidates' interaction

Some examples of good answers are the following:

Interlocutor	*In general, do you think leaders get enough respect in society?*
Candidate A	*Well, we've been talking about power and status, which could be construed as respect, couldn't it? So, in a way, there's this perception that leaders are the ones who have the greatest respect in society. But at the same time, I think they're also the ones who come under the closest scrutiny, although you might see it differently, Candidate B!*
Candidate B	*I was going to say the same thing, actually. And maybe the media, at least in some countries, take great delight in bringing them down. So we put leaders on a pedestal and then we end up disappointed when they don't meet our unrealistic expectations.*

In the answers above, we see great examples of interaction, linguistic proficiency and insightfulness. Candidate A reacts by showing how the interlocutor's question links back to an earlier discussion (*Well, we've been talking about power and status, which could be construed as respect, couldn't it?*). He/she then explicitly addresses the question (*So, in a way, there's this perception that leaders are the ones who have the greatest respect in society*) before suggesting a personal view on the subject (*But at the same time, I think they're also the ones who come under the closest scrutiny*). To finish, he/she invites Candidate B to participate by indirectly asking for his/her view (*...although you might see it differently!*) Candidate B then completely agrees with Candidate A (*I was going to say the same thing, actually.*) and then goes on to expand the answer with a specific example (*maybe the media, at least in some countries, take great delight in bringing them down. So we put leaders on a pedestal and then we end up disappointed when they don't meet our unrealistic expectations...*). The following example also shows some great interaction in Part 3:

Interlocutor	*It is sometimes said that the most effective leaders are invisible. Do you agree?*
Candidate A	*Wow, that's a tough one, to be honest. Erm... I'm not sure what that could mean. Does it mean they don't do much? Or that their actions have little impact? Well, that doesn't make sense because*

	the leaders obviously do make a difference. So I'd have to disagree because leaders are the driving force by definition. What's your opinion?
Candidate B	*Ah, well I'd interpret the saying differently. To me, what it's getting at is the idea that leaders tend to have more success when they let other people shine. They don't have to get the limelight all the time to drive their ideas forward. And there's probably some truth in that.*

In the previous example, we also see some interesting features. Candidate B starts by using a filler phrase to get more thinking time (*Wow, that's a tough one, to be honest,...*) and then expresses doubt about the interlocutor's question (*I'm not sure what that could mean...*). But instead of finishing the turn or asking for help, he/she reframes the question in a way that they can respond to. (*Does it mean they don't do much? Or that their actions have little impact?*). This gives Candidate A the chance to then provide a response (*Well, that doesn't make sense because the leaders obviously do make a difference. So I'd have to disagree because leaders are the driving force by definition...*). Finally, he/she asks for Candidate B's opinion. The latter shows how they viewed the interlocutor's question (*Ah, well I'd interpret the saying differently. To me, what it's getting at is ...*), using idiomatic language (*let other people shine ... get the limelight ...*) to expand on their answer and finishing by expressing some agreement (*There's probably some truth in that*).

Key thing to practise:

- Framing a subject or question (e.g. *Well, if you mean ... speaking from the perspective of ... in terms of ... I'd interpret that as being about ... to frame this within a broader/narrower context ... etc.*)

In the model answers provided by candidates, we can see that they:

- use C2-level structures
- sound very natural
- are well connected and organised
- tend to end with a question for the other candidate, which keeps the discussion going.

Finally, it is worth mentioning the presence, throughout the whole test, of collocations, idiomatic expressions and phrasal verbs typical of a native-like level of English. For example:

hanging out with ... kick off ... packed in like sardines ... driving force ... boils down to ... the buck stops with them ... the cut and thrust of ... plump for ... a small part of the story ... positive connotations ... put leaders on a pedestal ... let other people shine ... what makes people tick ... etc.

There is also a relevant reference that shows that the knowledge of the English language can transcend linguistic barriers and enter the cultural realm:

- Reference to a play on words (linking to the topic of transport): *Excuse the pun but there are several ways to navigate this issue...*

Other examples might include references to famous advertising slogans or well-known catchphrases made famous by entertainers. If used correctly and in a timely manner, this type of reference can cause a good impression on the examiners, helping candidates to obtain a better score. However, they should be used sparingly and could be viewed as inappropriate if touching on sensitive topics.

www.ingramcontent.com/pod-product-compliance
Lightning Source LLC
Chambersburg PA
CBHW081919090526
44591CB00014B/2397